'I went by the field of the slothful, and by the vineyard of the man void of understanding; And, lo, it was all grown over with thorns, and nettles had covered the face thereof, and the stone wall thereof was broken down. Then I saw, and considered it well: I looked upon it, and received instruction!

Proverbs, Chapter XXIV, verses 30-32

Text copyright ©
Susan Campbell 1983

Design copyright ©
Century Publishing Co. Ltd

Published in 1983 by
Century Publishing Co Ltd,
76 Old Compton Street,
London W1V 5PA

British Library Cataloguing
in Publication Data

Campbell, Susan
A calendar of gardeners' lore.
1. Gardening
I. Title
635 SB450.97

ISBN 0-7126-0247-X

Book design by
Nicholas Thirkell & Partners

Colour reproduction by
Alpha Reprographics Ltd
Harefield, Middlesex

Printed in Great Britain by
W.S. Cowell Ltd.,
Ipswich, Suffolk

SUSAN
CAMPBELL

A Calendar
OF
GARDENERS'
LORE
REVEALING
the Secrets of
THE
Walled Kitchen
Garden

Being an unrivalled collection
of useful *DIRECTIONS* &
OBSERVATIONS with the
addition of curious *FACTS* &
FANTASIES relating to the
History, Planning, Planting
& Management of *WALLED
KITCHEN GARDENS.*

CENTURY PUBLISHING
LONDON

In memory of H.B.S.B.
who died on November 14th 1980

Contents

The subject of this book is the walled *kitchen* garden. It is that square, secluded acre once described* as a garden *locked in high walls with its tradition of order, its Sunday silence.*

Alas, in most of those gardens today all that remains of that order is the walls themselves. Each quarter is thick with overgrown brambles; fruit trees stand in undisciplined gappy ranks, shaggy with neglect. The borders and alleyways which they once enclosed have been overlaid with blankets of couch-grass; hothouses are glassless and useless, their boilers sold for scrap.

The silence special to Sundays is now continuous. It stretches for month upon month of Sundays. The gardeners have all gone.

For me, walled kitchen gardens in full working order were (and are, when I find them,) places of great beauty; the productiveness and clandestine activity behind those walls is alluring. They also fall into a category of gardening which is quite distinct. They don't operate for profit, like market gardens, and they are not intended to help their owners eke out a modest living, like the vegetable patch in a cottage garden.

The walled kitchen gardens of vicarages, farmhouses and the houses of *gentlemen of small fortune* qualify for inclusion but

* Elizabeth Bowen, *Friends and Relations*, 1931

the most important gardens belonged to what Charles M'Intosh called (in 1853) *families of rank and fashion*. These families were expected to *indulge in all the luxuries of the table*. The horticultural ingenuity which enabled them to do this is what I find interesting. Their gardens provided them with an astounding variety of superb and exotic fruit and vegetables, as well as staples, all the year round. This produce was consumed by households which rarely seem to have consisted of less than two dozen people and were often considerably larger.

The owners of these gardens took as much pride in them as they did in their paintings, their furniture, their library, stables, farmlands or pleasure gardens. What is more, they would compete against their neighbours to produce the rarest, the newest, the earliest, the latest, the biggest and the best of luxuries. It is largely thanks to this amiable rivalry, combined with the challenge of growing curiosities from climates totally different from ours, that so many horticultural innovations and developments were made in the kitchen garden.

Those abandoned, solitary acres are monuments to an age of horticultural excellence and adventure. Their present decline is, as one old-fashioned gardener put it, 'all down to the accountants'. This book offers a few glimpses of life as it was in the walled garden, before the last of the ledger books was thrown onto the bonfire.

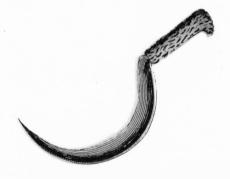

The Gard'ners' year is a circle as their labour is never at an end.

As in this one, many old *Gardener's Kalendars* and *Gardening Years* make November the first month; this is when the seed catalogues begin to arrive. It is also time to 'contrive and forecast' where and what you are to sow and plant. *Trench and fallow all your vacant grounds. Prepare and mix soils and composts thoroughly.* . . . The writer is John Reid, a Scot, and if you happen to live on a thoroughfare much used by horses, his advice is as good today as it was in 1683 . . . *miss not highway earth* [and] *the cleanings of streets* . . .

The earth in the gardens is now strip'd of all its ornaments, and the frost, which is often severe in this month, spares nobody's gardens, but unmercifully destroys all it meets with . . . be careful to preserve all those novelties which we have begun to advance by art . . . to avoid the displeasure of seeing perish in one bitter night what we have been labouring two or three months to advance . . . (Stephen Switzer, 1727) *Cover well your Artichoaks with long dung to defend them against Frosts; the want whereof lost almost all the Artichoaks in England, in the hard winter, 1683.* (John Worlidge, 1688)

The size and situation of the kitchen garden

A small 19th-century family of seven people (excluding servants) was thought to need about an acre of kitchen garden to keep them in fruit and vegetables all the year round. Four men could keep it going. A kitchen garden on a noble or ducal estate, such as Longleat, Chatsworth or Castle Howard would extend over about a dozen acres, with a correspondingly larger workforce. These huge gardens were subdivided by more walls into smaller compartments, to give extra shelter and more space for wall-fruit. The Duke of Portland's kitchen garden at Welbeck Abbey occupied 25 acres and was, until recently, the second largest kitchen garden in England. The largest was the Royal Kitchen Garden at Windsor, which covered 31 acres and employed between 36 and 48 men.

Fortunes were spent on providing walls, hothouses, water supplies, outbuildings and offices; more fortunes went on keeping them going. The site was carefully chosen and was sometimes changed quite radically. It was thought at one time (by Lancelot Brown among others) that the kitchen garden with its disciplined squares, straight lines and utilitarian aspect was too unsightly and (on account of the cabbages, onions, leeks and horse dung) too smelly to be situated, as it was in former times, close to the house. These moves were not always cosmetic; sometimes land further away, as at Longleat, was found to be of better quality, and better drained. The first and second Viscounts of Weymouth had, between 1680 and 1730, spent some £40,000 on the kitchen gardens, parterres and pleasure grounds at Longleat. They were laid out by London and Wise on the north and west sides of the house. That site, which was always clayey and marshy, is now occupied by the Sealion Pool, the Picnic area and the Wolves Wood. The kitchen gardens were moved some time between 1730 and 1758, to a hill top half a mile away.

Urine

To *cherrish an Apple Tree* Mascall advises *Throw al about your apple trees on the rootes thereof, the urine of old men, or of stale pisse long kept, they shall bring fruite much better*. . . This is good for vines as well; for plum trees you should try *the old pisse of old*

men, *and dregs of wine, diluted with two parts of water.* By the
nineteenth century, when the science of gardening was better
understood, Baron von Liebig (the discoverer of biochemistry
and the inventor, among other things, of meat extract) had
discovered that 'long kept' urine, whether of old or young men
had no advantage over fresh, which was preferable in any case as
it did not smell of ammonia. As for using it in the garden, it is
excellent; *the annual urine of two men contains sufficient mineral
food for an acre of land, and mixed with ashes will produce a fair
crop of turnips.* Perhaps gardeners who like to extinguish their
autumnal bonfires by pissing on them are not just doing it for
fun.

Beating barren trees

If your trees are still barren after medicinal treatment, try
violence. The tag:

> *A woman, a dog, and a walnut tree*
> *The more you beat them the better they be.*

may do some good to a walnut tree. Seemingly devastating
treatment such as root-pruning, bark ringing, notching and
nicking is all recommended practice for stimulating fruit trees
into bearing today – see the current edition of the Royal
Horticultural Society's *Fruit Garden Displayed* – so we should

not be surprised when we read of gardeners shooting barren apple trees or 'cutting their throats with a knife', with beneficial results.

Many old gardeners still like to bash a few nails into the trunk of a fruit tree, to 'buck it up' – some say they have to be copper nails. Others say copper nails are poisonous to a tree, so it's kill or cure. Margaret Baker, in her *Gardener's Folklore* (1977) wonders if these disturbances are useful because: a) they stimulate the flow of sap, which by its smell deters insect pests or b) by the battering and jarring, shakes hibernating insects from their resting places. Mutilation of roots and branches stimulates growth.anyway.

Young gardener's education

As for the young gardener, he will find this *one of the most disagreeable months . . . but he may console himself with the shortness of the day, and hail the approach of evenings when he may cast aside his wet dress and fortify his mind by converse with books.* J. C. Loudon (*Encyclopaedia of Gardening*, 1882) suggested Turton's *Linnaeus*; Galpine's *Flora Britannica*; Sowerby's *British Botany*, his *Mineralogy* and his *Zoology; an Introduction to Entomology; all new works on practical gardening, if possible, as they appear . . . and as many other works as the master may be pleased to deposit in the gardener's office, or lend from the library of the mansion.* By way of encouragement the head gardener *if he is of a humane and kind turn of mind* (which was by no means always the case) . . . *may assemble the men and also the women, and read aloud to, and expound to, or answer questions put by them; or he may cause them to read aloud to and question one another, in such a way as to blend entertainment with instruction.*

Peas and beans

Early peas and broad beans can be sown now. John Abercrombie, the eighteenth-century horticulturist, points out that *beans planted now often succeed better than those which were planted three weeks or a month sooner*, though in common with other gardening writers, he warns that their survival is chancy at this time of year. The bean he recommends is the Mazagan. It *comes in earliest, is a great bearer, a good bean for the table and most proper to be planted at this season.* The naturalist (and a contemporary of Abercrombie's) Gilbert White planted two rows of Mazagans in his garden at Selborne on November 2 1755. He says *they were never planted in England* before this date. He gathered his first crop from them on June 27th 1756. In 1900 the Mazagan bean was on its way out, condemned by William Robinson; *though recommended in every book on the subject, the Mazagan is for us the worst and most useless of its race.* He recommended waiting till February, then sowing long-pods. Nevertheless, the Mazagan bean was grown continually and enthusiastically until the 1930s, but by then plant breeders had evolved equally hardy, and equally early, long-podded beans. The Mazagan has now vanished completely from catalogues and gardening books. If you look in a modern atlas for the eponymous town in Morocco from which these beans originally

came the search will be equally fruitless; Mazagan is now called El-Jadida.

Forcing asparagus

Hot-bed frames and forcing houses, after a two-month spell of emptiness, were usually spruced up and got ready for use again by mid-November. Stephen Switzer, horticultural writer, garden planner, seedsman, gardener and an exact contemporary of Bach, Handel, Pope and Swift called November and December *a kind of artificial spring; for by means of hot-beds we have all or most of those things that the real spring produces; salletings such as lop-lettuces, chervil, cresses and mustard are weekly sown . . . as also mint (the season for lamb being now coming in).* (1727) The favourite forced delicacy was asparagus. To have it ready by Christmas, it was started in the second or third week of this month, though according to Abercrombie *many of the kitchen gardeners about London begin to make asparagus hot-beds about the middle or latter end of September . . . in order to have asparagus fit to gather by Lord Mayor's Day, which always happens in the second week in November.* Over two hundred years later boat-loads of frozen lamb are sent to us from the other side of the world; but it is doubtful if any of the asparagus one sees on sale at this time comes from anywhere within a thousand miles of Bow Bells and I have never bought fresh mint anywhere in mid-winter.

Thermostat

With every kind of electronic monitoring device, modern greenhouses can be left to look after themselves to a far greater extent than was the case even as recently as 1950. Then, weekend duties were still part of all gardeners' rotas. Watering, fuelling, and shading or ventilating the greenhouse were the top priorities, but automation in this department dates back as far as 1806. In that year James Kewley, a Manxman, fitted his *alarum thermometer* in his own greenhouse. It worked with balances and

wires, opening or closing windows, sashes, ventilators, steam-cocks, chimney-valves and dampers as required. If the desired temperature was exceeded it would set off an alarm bell in the head gardener's office, or, if necessary *in his room, in the night-time*. It was patented in 1816.

Cow-house vinery

The British are notorious for putting the comfort of their cats, dogs and horses before that of themselves, their wives, husbands, or children; it comes as no surprise therefore to learn that greenhouses had central heating before dwelling houses did. This luxury, unless you had coalmines of your own, could be expensive in terms of fuel bills (some hothouses required a temperature of 70°F all year round) but Mr Lawson of Tirydail near Llandeilo economised by combining his vinery with his cow-house. He wrote to the *Horticultural Magazine* on November 22 1851 as follows; *The cows are now housed for the winter in the cow-house vinery, and very pretty they look with a row*

of chrysanthemums on the wall in front of them, just coming into blossom. A scarlet geranium too . . ., trained on the same wall, looks very well and luxuriant. Fahrenheit's thermometer registered 10°F of frost last night outside; in the cow-house vinery it registered 37°F as the lowest point. We have laid planks across the tie beams, and loaded them with pots of calceolarias, geraniums, strawberries etc. The vines have grown extremely well and next year I intend to . . . let them bear a few bunches, as their bearing will be a test of success. Later on, fearing that cow heat might be insufficient, both for the animals themselves and his vines, Mr Lawson flued the walls *to have fire heat for the comfort of the cattle in case of very severe frost, and to prevent late-hanging fruit from becoming mouldy.*

Grapes preserved

There was endless discussion in the horticultural magazines of the late nineteenth century about the best way to preserve grapes. They could be left hanging on the vine, and would stay fresh all winter; as long as the vinery was kept cool, dry and well ventilated. At Panshanger, Hertfordshire, Earl Cowper's grapes were kept like this until February. Others preferred putting them first in soft paper, then into jars, with all airspace filled up by bran. The jars were sealed hermetically and either buried in the ground or stored in the fruit room. *My children* wrote E. P. Roe, author of *Success with Small Fruits* in 1880, *place a white mark against the days on which we unearth a jar of grapes.* This scheme is as old as the one recommended by Sir Hugh Plat, three years before the Gunpowder Plot, in his *Delightes for Ladies* (1602). *To keep clusters of Grapes until Easter . . . cut a branch of the vine with everie cluster, placing an apple at the end of the branch; now and then renewing those apples as they rot, and after hanging in a presse or cupboard . . . where the grapes might not freeze.* Lunar planters and gatherers should note that he also recommends cutting the bunches at full moon, (as does Pliny). Variations on this method are recorded until late in the nineteenth century; some sharpen the cut ends first, then sear them with a hot iron and push them into *mangold wurtzels or beetroots*, others used sealing wax to stop the ends. About 1870 the practice of 'bottling' grapes became fashionable in the fruit room, especially in the grander gardens, and most notably at Welbeck Abbey where in 1879 the Duke of Portland's gardener, Mr Tillery, kept two late white varieties of grape (Lady Downe's and Royal Vineyard) fresh in bottles until June. At Floors the gardener to another Duke (of Roxburgh) kept his Lady Downe's grapes until June 10, using burgundy bottles. The bottles were stored in a cool, dry fruit room, with plenty of fresh air circulating. They were filled with plain soft water, some kept it pure with a little charcoal, others added sugar. Clear glass bottles were preferred to coloured ones – they allowed the gardener to see when the water needed topping up. The grapes were left on the vine till Christmas, then cut with enough wood to reach to the bottom of the bottles and transferred to the fruit room. This method was still employed at Cornbury Park, Oxfordshire, in the 1950s. A piece of paper was hung behind each bunch of grapes to keep them away from the wooden shelf on which the bottles rested. Bottles especially designed for grapes are now collectors' items.

Boots

November can be windy, cold, frosty and wet. This is how gardeners made their boots waterproof before rubber wellingtons had been invented; 1 pint boiled linseed oil, ½ lb mutton suet, 6 oz clean beeswax, 4 oz resin, was melted and mixed well. While the mixture was still warm it was brushed 'plentifully' on to new boots and shoes while they were quite dry and clean. The leather stays soft. William Jones is the author of this recipe, which is to be found in a little book dated 1858 (*The Gardener's Receipt Book*) He adds: *New England fishermen have preserved their boots by this method for over a hundred years. They can stand in the water hour after hour without inconvenience.*

Odd jobs

Sweep and cleanse your garden-walks, and all other places, from Autumnal leaves, the last time. Get a dish of water, or moistened cloth in your greenhouse, so that you may know if it is freezing. (1691) See to your seeds . . . fill the ice house if the frost is sufficiently strong . . . examine such bunches of grapes and branches of plums and currants as you have hung up to preserve the fruit . . . paint and cleanse forcing houses . . . protect any outstanding edible roots with litter or leaves. . . (1822)

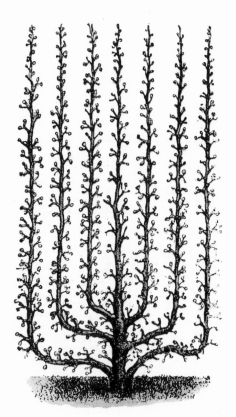

This month (the days being at the shortest) is the darkest of the whole year, . . . Sometimes the ground is frozen up, so that little can be done in the garden; and at other times there are hard rains, and thick stinking fogs, which render it very uncomfortable stirring abroad, and are very injurious to plants. (Philip Miller, *The Gardeners Kalendar*, 1734, 3rd edition)

The garden walls

Walls encompass everything in the kitchen garden. Four square, pockmarked with holes from the nails of generations of gardeners, too high to see over, punctuated very occasionally by a solid wooden door, or, where the aspect opens onto the formal garden, by a wrought iron gate with ornamental piers, they make the kitchen garden into a secret citadel or fortress and have themselves been the subject of some curious experiments. Early gardeners in the British Isles were quick to see that plants growing against a south-facing wall were afforded extra warmth and protection; how to improve on the situation was to occupy a series of innovative horticulturalists from Hugh Plat (c. 1552-1609) to William Robinson (1838-1935) (his steeply sloping vegetable garden at Gravetye Manor is oval). The chief aim was to increase the amount of warmth a wall might provide. An ingenious idea was recorded by Sir Hugh Plat before he died, but it was not published till 1653. He made the

[22]

suggestion that curved tabernacles of lead, iron or tin garnished with glasses of steel or crystalline could be built behind fruit trees, (Olive, Lemon or Pomegranate), to reflect the heat of the sun. He also made a more important suggestion: *if these walls did stand so conveniently as they might also be warmed with kitchen fires, as serving the Backs unto chimneys*. The idea of a flued wall was born, but none are mentioned or recorded until John Laurence's *Fruit Garden Kalendar* of 1718. He says in his introduction that although he hasn't seen such a wall *by the Help of Stoves at convenient Distances, and cavities in the Structure of the Wall to convey the Heat to all parts, the desirable Purpose of early, large and good Grapes must be attained . . .* He adds that this need not be expensive *in a country of coals, where a wagon load of the small sort may be had and brought for two or three shillings*. He also suggests laying a heap of fresh dung behind the walls, which would *have the same effect as a gentle fire*. The first mention of a flued wall appeared in Switzer's *Practical Fruit Gardener* of 1731. This was not only flued, but sloped. The wall lay at an angle of 45° and flues ran under the floor (as they did in Evelyn's hothouse of 1691) as well as along the back wall.

Fixtures and fastenings for wall-fruit trees

The use of iron nails was frowned on by Stephen Switzer, who preferred *little round wooden peggs, made of Heart of Oak, drove into the wall between the bricks, to which may be ty'd all the small Branches with the Juncus or Small Rush that grows in watery places*. The larger branches should be fixed to larger pegs, and tied with withies or basket rods of osier. The advantage of the rush and withy ties over *lists or shreds* made of cloth or leather was that they were cheaper and less harmful to the tree. They would break as the branches grew. They were also quicker to unlace, should you need to re-align a peach tree, for example. He preferred wooden pegs because they too were cheaper, as well as long-lasting

D e c e m b e r

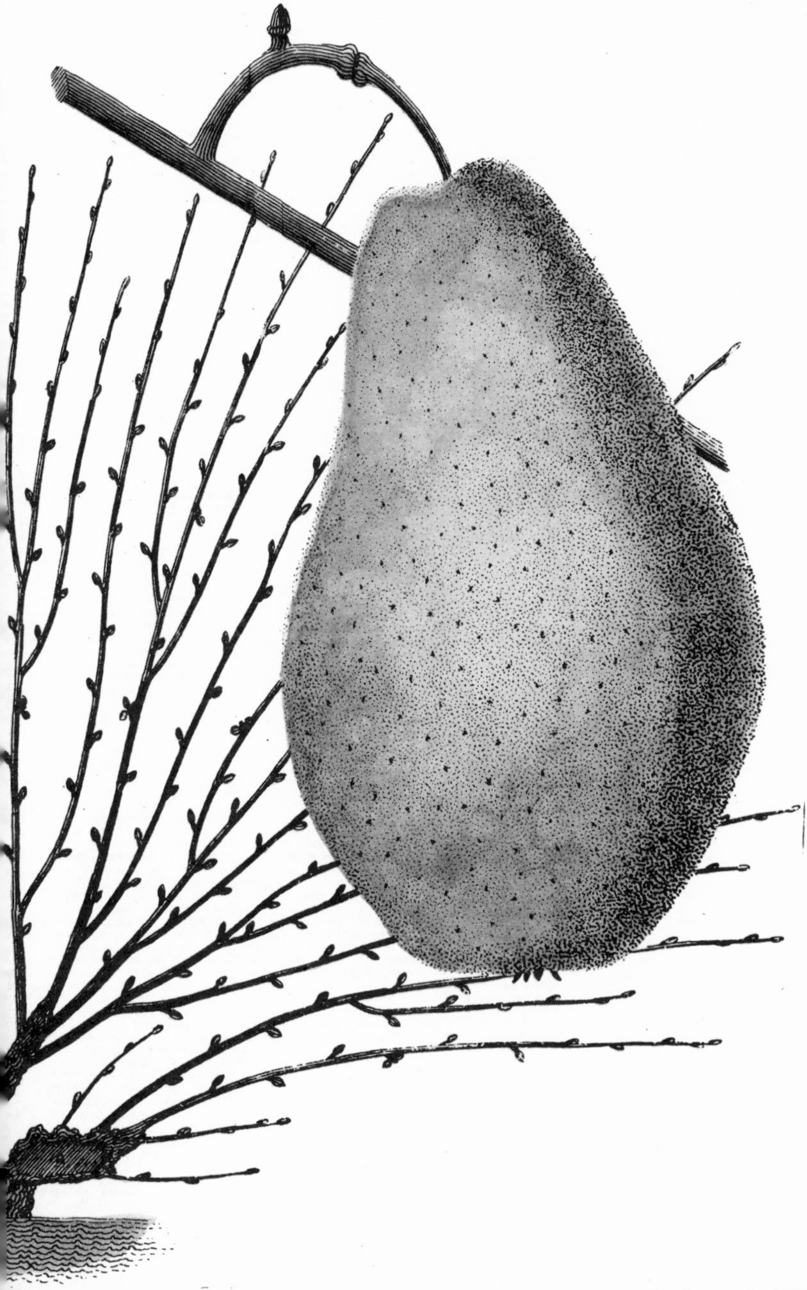

and wouldn't *gall or fret the young branches as rusty nails will with their square edges.* (1731)

A lattice made of heart of oak was the fixture best liked by Jean de la Quintinie, gardener to Louis XIV at Versailles, in 1673. Failing that he suggests poles painted *mountain green* fixed vertically and horizontally to iron spikes or hooks. He disliked wires attached to flat-headed nails; they hurt the trees. *Others*, he notes, *stick the bones of horses, oxen or sheep, in straight lines along the wall, and tie branches to them.*

To nail a tree to a wall

You can start nailing trees at Michaelmas (29th Sept) and continue till early April. The *great annual labour of nailing should be carried on whenever the weather is mild enough. It is a job much better performed when one is not finger-cold*, says the *Gardener's Chronicle* for December 1884. John Reid (*The Scots Gard'ner*) used *double plancher-nails and the tags of hats (which is better than leather)*. He made his tags half an inch wide and up to 5 inches long, folded them and made a slit near the ends, to slip over the nail; then he spread the tree, laying, plying and nailing every branch by itself, all at equal distances from one another, with none crossing. He cut away *the superfluous, those that will not ply easily and the exuberant or lustie that rob the rest . . . drive the nail but halfway in, and on the upper side of the branch, else it will lean and gall*. At every nailing he altered the old nails, and took care not to pinch the young branches by making the tags too tight. Finally, he could stand back and admire his beautifully trained fan-shaped pear or peach; *Well plyed trees will appear like peacock's train spread.* (1683)

Moveable fruit walls

The most impracticable idea for a fruit wall must go to the mathematician Nicolas Fatio de Douillier FRS. Looking somewhat like a giant radar screen, but convex and trapezoid, rather than concave and circular, this wall was designed to slope upwards towards the sun, and rotate with it throughout the day.

Serpentine walls

Suffolk is the county which abounds in serpentine garden walls. The legend attached to those built in the early 19th century is that they were built by French prisoners taken in the Napoleonic Wars. But the oldest serpentine wall still standing is possibly the one at West Horsley Place in Sussex, which is shown on a plan of the Estate dated 1736. Pepys mentions going

to see Lord Hinchingbrooke's garden at Huntingdon, where the *crooked wall on the mount* was being brought *to a shape*, in 1663, though it is not clear if it was built for fruit, or just for pleasure. Crinkle-Crankle, zig-zag, ribbon or serpentine walls have one great advantage over straight walls; they are cheaper to build, as they can be only one brick thick. They can also be made of thatched mud or chalk, and usually house one fruit tree in each embrasure. Their only disadvantage is that the wind tends to buffet the trees by being reflected off each curve, or as John Reid, *The Scots Gard'ner* put it in 1683: *the wind being pent up occasions squirls and retards the ripening of the fruits there planted.*

The ice house

Somewhere in the park or gardens surrounding any large old mansion there is sure to be an ice house. This came under the gardener's domain and was usually positioned near a lake or pond, but on ground high enough for water from melted ice to drain out of it. At least two-thirds of the structure was below ground, with a treble-doored entrance facing north, near the top. Trees were sometimes planted on top of them to provide shade. They were built of stone or brick. The ice was collected as soon as it had frozen thickly enough for a man to stand on it. The ice house at Chatsworth is appropriately enough beside the Ice Pond, which is well known to Hunter Trial enthusiasts. This house was built in 1693 which makes it one of the oldest in the country. (The earliest reference to an English ice house is 1666, when a thatched 'Snow-well' was sunk at St James's Palace). The ice house at Chatsworth was still in use until the outbreak of World War II. It is thanks to the first-hand recollections of two of the staff there that Mr Denis Fisher, the one-time Comptroller has been able to record in detail how the ice house was filled. First, as soon as a frost looked imminent, the Ice Pond was flooded. Water was sluiced through it until all debris such as leaves and twigs had been washed away. The outlet to the pond was then closed off, and a gamekeeper was posted to keep birds and animals away. As soon as the ice was an inch thick, work could begin. The men wore scrupulously clean boots and worked with scrupulously clean tools. They cut a margin of ice two or three feet wide from the edge of the pond. The main part of the ice was then broken up and dragged towards the ice house at the northern end of the pond. Here it was smashed into smaller pieces with wooden mallets and pushed through a chute at the top of the ice house into the empty chamber. A 'breaker' was sent down a ladder to smash the ice into smaller pieces. (Loudon says the particles should not be larger than sand or salt.) It was packed so tightly that it eventually formed a solid block. Every time the pond froze the ice house was topped up. When the house was full the ice lasted all summer, but obviously even in Derbyshire, winters were sometimes too mild for ice to form. For this reason some places had ice houses big enough for supplies to last two or even three years. Ice was mainly used for the making of frozen desserts and to cool drinks, or for serving luxuries such as jellies, pineapples or oysters. It was dug out of the ice chamber like coal and sent in bags to the kitchens.

The ice house as a cooler

A letter to *The Times*. September 1980. From Mr Graham Binns.

Sir, There is an ice house cut into the rock at the back of Ruskin's old home, Brantwood. When I was a boy an old outdoor servant of Ruskin called Wilkinson, lived at the lodge there. He told me that when Ruskin became crotchety and disturbed towards the end of his life, Mrs Severn his cousin would have him wheeled in there to cool off. Yours faithfully. . .

Ruskin died in 1900, aged 81. Brantwood is near Coniston in the Lake District and now belongs to the Brantwood Educational Trust. The story, as visitors to the ice house will see for themselves, must be apocryphal; there are far too many steps for a wheelchair to be taken in, let alone a wheelchair with an obstreperous person in it. What is true is that Ruskin began building the ice house himself, though like many other projects he began, other people had to finish it for him.

Onions and the shortest day

With many gardeners it was, and still is, traditional to plant

[29]

certain kinds of onion on the shortest day and to reap them on the longest. Christmas Day is still exhibition onion-sowing day for some amateurs and cottage gardeners, but for older, professional gardeners, Christmas Day was one of their two precious, paid holidays in the year (the other was Good Friday). They sowed or planted their onions on St Thomas's Day, December 21st.

Potato onions look and grow rather like shallots; that is to say they grow clusters of new bulbs around the parent bulb and grow under the ground. They were popular with Victorian gardeners in the West Country, and were last heard of (c. 1950) in Co. Kerry. They have a strong flavour, and will keep until February.

Bird scarers, scarecrows, feathers and bells

Hungry pigeons regard our winter kales and cabbages as a nice alternative to their natural but diminishing winter diet; they have to be scared off. Mr Clinkscale, the gardener at Cringletie House Hotel, near Peebles, in Scotland, sticks feathers in the ground among the vegetables which the pigeons seem to like most. They then regard the patch as the territory of another bird, and leave it alone. At Christmas Mr Clinkscale is given huge white turkey feathers by the butcher. He tells inquisitive visitors who ask him what the feathers are for that he's growing turkeys.

London and Wise suggest combining wing feathers with carrier's bells, hung from a horizontal pole; *Which, by means of the wind coming to ring and the feathers turning nimbly round at the same time, the birds will be so frightened, as well at the noise as the sight, that they will immediately fly away.* A similar arrangement, a potato stuck with feathers and hanging from a string, like the bait on a fishing line, was recommended as a *very good and simple scarecrow* by M'Intosh in the first edition of his *Book of the Garden* in 1828. But by the edition of 1885 he calls it no more than *a potato dangler* and *a sorry preventive.*

[30]

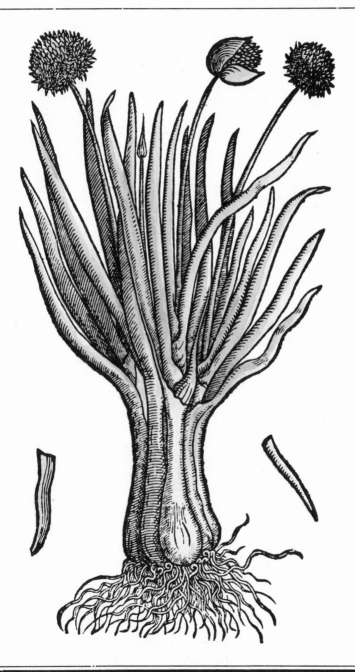

To destroy vermin and keep out intruders

Larger animals head a string of *Naturall things, externally hurting orchards* in William Lawson's *New Orchard and Garden,* 1621: group one (Beasts) lists *Deere, Goats, Sheep, Hare, Cony, Cattell, Horse*; group two (Birds) *Bulfinch, Thrush, Blackbird, Crow, Pye (Maw Pie)*; other evils are –

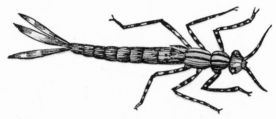

Winds, Cold, Trees, Weeds, Wormes, Mowles, Filth, Poysonfull Smoke, a careless Master, and indiscreet, negligent or no Keeper. Remedies for group one include *a faire and swift Greyhound, a stone-bow, a gun and if need require an apple with an hook for a Deere and an Hare-pipe for an Hare.* Against birds, he says *to take a stone bow, a Piece, especially if you have a Musket or a Spar-hawke in winter to make the Black-bird stoope into a bush or hedge. Justice and liberality* will put away cruel neighbours and *A brood of nightingales will sing and eat caterpillars.*

For mice, various ingenious traps can be set, including narrow-necked, baited jars dug in the ground, (the mice fall in and then can't get out) and a delicately balanced brick which falls on the mouse as soon as it nibbles at a string of germinating peas; (they like these better than dried ones).

How to have mistletoe

Although it is a parasite, few gardeners are so punctilious as to remove mistletoe from their fruit trees; for one thing it is always welcomed as a Christmas decoration, for another, if there is lots of it, it is as saleable a commodity as fruit. Its growth is encouraged by Loudon; propagate it in February by pushing a bruised berry into a slit *like that made in budding*, on the bark of apple, pear, thorn or *almost any tree*. There is a belief that the seed will only germinate if it has first been passed through the digestive system of a bird – the mistlethrush is the obvious favourite for this theory. But Walker's *Essays on Natural History* show that *the digestive juices of the bird destroy the vegetative powers of the seed*. So it is likely that where the mistlethrush is concerned, he eats the berries and, in wiping the stickiness from his beak by rubbing it against the tree, plants the seed as efficiently as any gardener.

How to find mistletoe

By sitting uppon a hill late in an evening, neere a wood, in a fewe nights a firedrake (Will o' the wisp) will appear; marke where it lighteth, and there you shall find an oake with Mistletoe therein, at the roote wherof there is a misselchild, whereof many strange things are conceived (Hugh Plat, 1608)

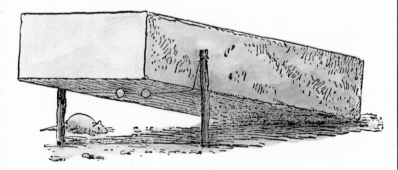

Odd jobs

Work to be done in the late afternoon, *by candlelight till supper time . . . . making of straw screens and coverings for the fruit trees, or [for] those pease and beans that are grown high above the ground; roping of onions, placing roots, endive etc., in cellars, in sand.* (1727) *Turne and refresh your fruit in a clear serene day. Sharpen and mend tools. Gather oziers and hassell rods and make baskets in stormy weather. Cover your water pipes with leitter lest the frosts do crack them; feed weak bees.* (1683) *Be careful now to keep the doors and windows of your conservatories well matted and guarded from the piercing air; for your oranges are now put to the test. . . look to your fountain pipes. . . . remember it in time and the advice will save you both trouble and charge.* (1691)

This month is generally the coldest month of the year, and not seldom lock'd up with Frosts, or the Gardens as well as the Fields, covered with Snow, that little can be done in the Garden . . . it is not sage to sow any manner of seeds (except in hot Beds) least a sharp fit of Cold chill them in their Milk, after they have swelled in the Earth and began to chitt, as many seeds are apt to do as soon as they are in the Ground. (John Worlidge, *Gardener's Monthly Directions*, 1688)

Jan. 20. Tuesday . . . Last night was the severest we have had yet. It froze so sharp within doors, that the Milk in the Milk-pans in the Dairy, was froze in a Mass. . . Jan. 21. Wednesday . . . so cold that the Poultry kept in the Cart-shed and obliged to be driven out to be fed. . . Jan. 25. Sunday . . . It froze last night the Chamber Pots above Stairs. (From Parson Woodforde's *Diary*, 1795)

In January 1763, Gilbert White had, as usual made his hot-beds for the cucumbers, and sown seeds, even though: *Jan. 11. Fierce frost still, but not very windy. . . The Thames it seems is so frozen that fairs have been kept on it; and the ice has done great damage to the ships below Bridge . . . covered the bulbs with straw, and the artichokes . . . lined the cucumr. bed a little; the plants look pretty well.* This frost had begun on Christmas Day and lasted till January 28th.

Grafting

Grafting takes place in the dead of winter, before the sap begins to rise and before buds start swelling. The gardener will have his stocks already rooted and waiting; with surgical precision,

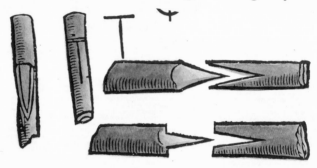

speed and cleanliness he makes cabbalistic-looking cuts in them, and binds his young scions to them. It is one of the most creative and rewarding jobs in the garden, and one which seems to inspire poets as well. The following verses are an extract from *Upon love fondly refused for conscience sake* by a poet not usually associated with gardening – Lord Rochester (1647-1680)

> *If the fresh trunk have sap enough to give*
> *That each insertive branch may live*
> *The gard'ner grafts not only apples there*
> *But adds the warden and the pear*
>
> *The peach and apricot together grow,*
> *The cherry and the damson too,*
> *'Till he hath made by skilful husbandry*
> *An entire orchard of one tree. . .*

Tools for grafting

A toole of Ebony or Box is better to open the barke than a toole of iron, if you would graft a scion between the barke and the tree.
(1608)

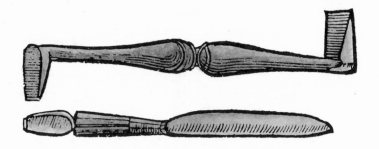

Grafting apples onto crab stocks

An apple grafted on a crab not only contributes to the duration of the tree, but by the inter-mixture of that sharpness with which the Crab is naturally endu'd, gives that Briskness of taste so valuable in Apples, whilst an Apple grafted on an Apple eats sickish and pall'd, little better than a Turnip. (Switzer, 1752)

Fruit and vegetables out of season

For the ambitious gardener, there's nothing more satisfying than being able to produce fruit and vegetables months out of season; and as long ago as 1822, in the reign of George IV, any gardener worthy of his post in a well-run gentleman's establishment was expected to supply his master's kitchen with an assortment of the following in January: — kidney beans, seakale, small salads such as cresses, lettuces, radishes, lamb's lettuce, sorrel, endive, celery, (the last three cut as seedling leaves); herbs such as parsley, tarragon, chervil, fennel; rhubarb, mushrooms, pineapples, winter melons, grapes, new potatoes, strawberries, cucumbers (a few), oranges, olives, pomegranates, Malay apples, *Eugenia malacceusis* (a rose-scented oval fruit from the South Seas), loquats, lichees, yams, and Spanish potatoes (sweet potatoes).

Deficiencies in the Royal Kitchen Gardens

Not every gentleman's gardener in the early nineteenth century was capable of producing all these luxuries . . . Surprisingly, and most lamentably, some of the least capable of all were employed in the Royal Kitchen Gardens by their Royal Highnesses, King William IV and Queen Adelaide. Their Majesties lived mainly at Buckingham Palace and Windsor Castle, spending the spring and summer in London, and autumn and winter at Windsor. The Royal Table was supplied with fruit and vegetables from kitchen gardens at Kensington Palace, Hampton Court, Kew Palace and Windsor Castle itself. Between them, these gardens encompassed 64 acres. Nevertheless, every year the Lord Steward was obliged to buy considerable quantities of fruit at seasons when the gardens ought to be in full supply . . . *gooseberries, currants, pears and peaches were bought yearly. . . Not a strawberry or a grape was furnished by the Royal Forcing Houses in the months of January or February, 1837 and scarcely even in March.* In July 1837, grapes were bought in spite of the 30,000 square feet of glass sheltering the Royal Vineries. In the winter of the same year it had been necessary to buy in seakale, parsley, spinach, celery and asparagus, productions of the 64 forcing houses falling much too far short of what was needed. On the other hand there were excesses. It was quite difficult even for a Royal Household

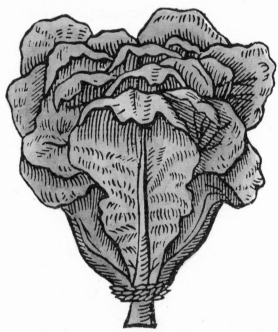

with 160 servants to dispose in one month (August 1837) of 221 pineapples, 600 pecks of kidney beans and 2,900 cucumbers. In January 1838, seven months after the accession of Queen Victoria, the House of Lords set up an inquiry into the running of the Royal Kitchen Gardens. The *Gardener's Gazette* of the time was in no doubt as to what they would find. A visitor to the gardens of Buckingham Palace itself would be hard put to it to find a *garden within ten miles of London, public or private, Kew only excepted, so ill conducted, in such wretched bad order. . . he will stare at finding only seven or eight bungling old men, who, worthy as they may be in other respects, are no more fit for the duties of gardeners than Loudon* [of *Encyclopaedia* fame] *is fit for a lighterman or Mr Aiton* [in charge of Kew] *for a dancing master.* Their sobriety was also in question. The inquiry found that *the Royal Gardens have a bad name – no applications are now made to them for gardeners to go all over the country, as was formerly the case. Public confidence is withdrawn; discipline is lax.* So a new garden was planned for Windsor, to be financed by the rents from 33 new houses on the site of the old Kensington Palace Kitchen Gardens (now Kensington Palace Gardens). It cost £50,000, occupied 31 acres and was the wonder of its age.

The new Royal Kitchen Gardens at Windsor, 1853

Queen Victoria's new kitchen garden was in full production by 1853. It was all that the most advanced and productive garden of its age could be. It was laid out so that the Queen could enter it from the park *through a modest but massive gateway* in a pony-carriage. Before her stretched a wide terrace, 1,132 feet long and 20 feet wide. On the right was a continuous range of glass houses stretching from one end to the other, interrupted only by the gardener's house in the middle. The left side of the terrace was lined with wide flower beds, and beyond it lay the kitchen garden. Enormous artificial stone eagles surmounted the ends of each twelve foot high wall. From the gardener's house, where two rooms were set aside for Royal visits, Her Majesty could survey the ranks of fruit and vegetables as she  might a durbar or an army, or the fleet. In order not to obstruct the view from the terrace with tall espaliers, as was usual in this sort of garden, plums, apples, pears and cherries of a dwarf kind were trained over four foot high arched trellises so that each walk was bordered by a low tunnel of fruit. The view was bounded by an east wall covered in pears, a south wall devoted to apricots, peaches, nectarines and cherries, and a west wall supporting plums. The north side of the south wall was used for currants and gooseberries. On the outer, or slip wall there were figs and mulberries.

An odd use for watering cans

From a fictitious pocket memorandum book, such as a young gardener's apprentice is supposed to keep:

Jan 28th 1821. Parsneps – Gurkin O'Doolittle caught distilling parsnep whiskey in the tan-shed; discharged without a character. His still, two watering pots placed top to top, and closed with a wet cloth; the top kept cool by pouring water on it. (J. C. Loudon, *Encyclopaedia of Gardening*, 1830 edn)

Loudon was trying to encourage the powers of observation in the young, rather than drunkenness.

A winter salad, 1722

Like Evelyn, Stephen Switzer compiled very precise lists, with the proper quantities, for salads at various seasons. This is his *good sallet* for January, February or March:–

4 roots sellery, 3 roots endive, 2 roots succory (chicory), 2 roots fennel, 3 roots rampion (*campanula rapunculus*). All blanched. Corn salad or lamb's lettuce, lop lettuce. A 'handsome gripe of each'. Raddish and cresses – 3 pinches (leaves). Turnep and mustard – 2 pinches (leaves), sorrel, cherwithe (chervil?), burnet, rocket. A large pinch of each. Tarragon, mint – 12 tops each, 10-12 shallots or small onions 'with their green', 1-2 cabbage lettuces 'if you have them'.

These items were to be gathered in a special basket, which kept each one *entirely separate because some gentlemen love one kind of sallet, and some another*. It was *divided into eight or ten small squares or cells* with *three or four larger, long divisions or cells which are placed in the middle, to hold the roots of sellery, endive, fennel etc in the winter, or the different kinds of cabbage lettuce in the summer*. Having plucked the salad early in the morning (with the dew still on it), left it in a cool place, carefully washed, trimmed and arranged it *in a method and order, that when well done is both pleasing to the master as well as the gardener*, the gardener could congratulate himself on creating *as beautiful a dish as any comes to a nobleman's or gentleman's table.*

Advice to the young gardener

The gardener, during this month, does not labour in the garden more than five hours a day; allowing one hour more for early and late attendance on hot-house fires, and seven hours for sleep, there remains eleven hours for personal improvement. Let the young gardener, who is ambitious of distinguishing himself from the common clay of his profession, not let one of these hours run to waste. (J. C. Loudon, *Encyclopaedia of Gardening*, 1830 edn)

Odd jobs

Set traps to destroy vermine, for in frosty weather they will easily be taken by a Bait. . . pick snails out of the crevices in the walls and other close places where they go for shelter. (1688) *'A paste to Kill Vermin' – course Honey, wherein is mingled Green-glass, beaten, with Copris to be laid near their haunts.* (1691)

In over-wet, or hard weather, cleanse, mend, sharpen and prepare garden-tools. Turn up your Beehives and sprinkle them with a little warm and sweet Wort; do it dextrously. (1691) *Feed weak bees, also you may remove them.* (1683) *Paste strips of paper where the wind blows in to greenhouses. Scrape moss from all trees. Wheel dung in frosty weather, when other work cannot be done.* (1779) *Make straw mats, and wooden cases.* (1706)

Even deep snow gives time for cleaning, thrashing and sorting of seeds, preparing stakes and pea-sticks, tying mats, sorting bulbs. . . (1833)

*Bees come out of their hives,
the partridge begins to pair, the
blackbird whistles and the field and wood-
larks sing; the hen sits.* (Loudon's *Encyclopaedia of
Gardening*, 1830 edn)

February 14, 1767. *A very wet season. House-pidgeons
begin to lay. Cast dung in the farm yards.* (Gilbert White's *Garden
Kalendar*)

*Now the weather begins to alter . . . . the inclining of the Sun to
the Vernal Equinox doth produce a moderation of past colds, and
encourage the ingenious gardener to trim his trees, and stir his
ground, mixing his rotten dung in the digging thereof for the setting
and sowing of Beans, Pease, Carrots, Parsnips, Onions, Parsley,
Spinage, Asparagus, Anniseeds, Corn-Sallet, Fennel. . .* (John
Worlidge, *The Gardener's Monthly Directions*, 1688)

Garden hierarchy

In large nineteenth- and twentieth-century gardens the head
gardener was king. He was on a par with the head coachman or
chauffeur, the butler and the cook. He had his own house.
Below him he had three foremen; the 'inside foreman', in
charge of all the glasshouses; the kitchen garden foreman, in
charge of all outside fruit and vegetables, and the pleasure
garden foreman. In large gardens there might be a fourth
foreman, or forester, in charge of woods and plantations. These
men all lived in other garden houses or in the nearby village.

Each foreman had a staff of journeymen, apprentices and garden boys. The boys, aged from 13 to 15, were local and lived mostly at home, as did the apprentices (also known as labourers or improvers who were aged between 16 and 20). The journeymen might be any age between 20 and 60 and were qualified workers.

The head gardener's house

In large, grand gardens, such as Floors, Chatsworth, Windsor, Welbeck, Mellerstain or Castle Howard, the head gardener's house sat either at the entrance to, or in the centre of, the kitchen gardens, like a little mansion in an estate of its own. On humbler estates the head gardener's house was usually tacked on to the kitchen garden walls; the wall facing into the garden would have few windows in it to avoid wasting valuable wall-fruit space. The other, outward face would, to all intents and purposes look like an ordinary cottage. The nearer it was to the hothouses and forcing grounds, the better. The  gardener needed to keep a constant watch on these, not only because the temperatures, ventilation and watering needed attention at all times, but also, by his nearness to deter thieving.

The grandest gardeners would also need an office. The seed rooms and various other store rooms might form part of this complex, but normally they were built behind the greenhouses among the 'back sheds'.

The duties of the head gardener

Evelyn's *Directions to his gardener at Say's Court*, written in 1687, could have been used by any gardener without a word altered for the next one hundred years.

Every Monday Morning, he must walk about the whole place

to observe what needs doing, what is amisse, before he does any other work . . . Make regular checks on beehives, seed and root boxes; clean, sharpen and repair tools in wett weather and put away every night. Stir heaps of dung and mould; clip hedges, mow lawns, prune fruit and murral trees and vines when stated. Ask every night what rootes, salading, garnishing will be needed next day, and bring it to cook in the morning and informe her from time to time what garden provision and fruite is ripe and in season to be spent . . . Gather and bring in all fruit . . . He may not dispose of any fruit or sell any vegetables, flowers or plants without first asking leave of master or mistress. He must show broken and worn out tools to the master before buying new ones. He is also given *a paper book to note what, when and where he sows and plants, and register for the success of tryalls.* The 19th-century head gardener kept account books for Time, Cash and Forest work, and notebooks relating to the sowing and reaping of crops, trenching, produce and weather as well as a register of hothouse temperatures, records of plant growth and various other memo books. He did have some perks, too. He could keep the money from the fruit and vegetables that he was allowed to sell, wear a bowler hat, and, of course, smoke. There was also, after the establishment of the Royal Horticultural Society's annual Flower Show, the great privilege of accompanying his master and produce to London in top hat, tails and white gloves. The wife went too.

The inside foreman

The inside foreman was the head gardener's second in

command, and a position to be held by anyone who aspired to get to the top. Mr Miller Gault, now in his eighties, was inside foreman at Holkham Hall before World War II and Head Gardener at Regent's Park, London after it. At Holkham it was his job to collect and arrange all the fruit and flowers for the table. As at every establishment of quality, the table decorations were changed three times a day, once for breakfast, once for lunch, and once for dinner. There would be a floral centre-piece, and a trailing plant such as *smilax, hoya bella* or *hoya canosa* in tracery work round each place. The gardeners preferred to have a white cloth on the table, it showed up the arrangements better than mahogany. Fruit lay in a basket, or on a silver dish with a pretty bed made of decorative vine or variegated pelargonium leaves. Each variety was labelled with a card, with its name in the gardener's best copperplate handwriting.

Mrs Beeton's table decorations

In Winter, apples or oranges are arranged in pyramids, with bay or holly leaves to decorate.

A dish of mixed summer fruit is arranged in layers, with due regard to contrast of colour and well separated by plenty of leaves between each layer. White cherries at the bottom, then red raspberries, then white currants, and at the top some fine scarlet strawberries.

In September and October *a high raised appearance can be given in the following manner. A pineapple, crown uppermost, is placed in a tumbler, in the centre of the dish. The tumbler is surrounded with a thick layer of moss, and whatever fruit is in season is laid upon it. The moss economises on the amount of fruit needed, and also gives the dish a better shape. Grapes should be placed on top of the fruit, with a portion of some of the bunches hanging over the sides in a negligé sort of manner, which takes off the formal look of the dish. (Mrs Beeton's Household Management,* 1860)

It was considered very elegant in Mrs Beeton's day to have all kinds of fruit brought to table still growing, in pots. Vines, figs, apples, pears, nectarines, peaches and strawberries were the favourite fruits for this treatment.

A great fall of snow

The gardener should never be fooled into thinking that because the early and mid-parts of winter were mild, the end of it will be the same. I am writing this in mid-February. On my desk are daffodils picked from the garden after the warmest January for years and the first snow of the winter is just starting to fall.

In 1813 at Earnshill, near Curry Rivel on the edge of Sedge Moor in Somerset, the gardener to the Combe family had much the same experience. The story is told in a notebook of the kind that was usually sent once a week between master and gardener in this sort of establishment. It is tall and narrow. Deliveries, orders and queries are written on the left-hand side, comments and answers from either party go on the right. Thus: *Sent in the B[asket] 29th December, Savoy Greens, Endive, Celery, Parsley, Broccoli, Horseradish, 2 Fowls, one Turkey, 3 Rabbits, 2 woodcocks, one partridge, one Pheasant. All arrived safe.*

From this it looks as if the poultry yard and game larder were situated near the kitchen garden; there was clearly a root cellar and fruit house because: *Sent in 2 baskets 12 January, Carrots, Parsnips, Onions, 6 Dozen Baking Apples, 8 Dozen Table Apples, 2 Dozen Eggs, Greens, Savoys, one Turkey, 2 Fowls, 2 Rabbits, some Pickled Pork, 2 Shapes.* But. . . *We have a great fall of snow here I could not get Celery or Parsley or Endive.*

Then follows an order in what is possibly the housekeeper's writing: *Send next week. . . Scorzonera, a small branch of Laurel and Bay-Myrtle Heath and anything else for the Epergne not forgetting the arbutus fruit and flowers — Jane to send one of the small hams, 2 chickens the best she has got, large fowl and two large rabbits and the large turkey.*

The next message, dated 9th February is in the gardener's writing; . . .*I sent you some Laurel and the only things I could pick instead of flowers as all the plants in the Greenhouse look as if they was quite dead with the frost.*

The master is unfortunately away; possibly the whole family is spending the winter with him at Bath — it would certainly explain why the amounts 'sent' are so large; but to return to the garden; the next entries are in the master's writing; *I would have none of the green plants that are dead thrown away till my return Feb 19.*
How many birds did you kill in the snow and frost?
(I have killed a good many blackbirds and small birds.)
What precautions did you use to prevent the frost injuring the greenhouse plants?
(I put litter before the door and kept a fire to it.)

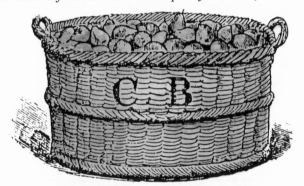

Cabbages, – cut and come again

In gardens where there is space to spare it is not necessary to dig the ground over for the next crop as soon as an old one has finished and you can leave the stumps of cabbages to grow again. But *observe to cut them sloping, with the slope or cut towards the South; as also to cut away from the stalk all the bottom leaves, to give liberty for the free growth of their sprouts, which are preferable to the cabbages themselves, and will plentifully furnish your table till the middle of April.* The sloping cut is to protect the stump from

rain and snow, which might rot it if it was able to settle. (Batty
Langley, *New Principles of Gardening*, 1728) Batty Langley's
favourite cabbages were the Sugar Loaf, the early white
Battersea, the French cabbage and the Savoy. They were all
firm, close and very large, yet very light. Top favourite was the
*curled Savoy, yellow in the middle, environed with deep green
curdled leaves is, of all others, the most beautiful, sweetest, and
despises the severity of our winter's frosts, which other kinds will
not.*

Circumposition

Now is the season for circumposition by Tubs or Baskets of Earth,
according to Evelyn's *Kalendarium Hortense* of 1691. This is a
seventeenth-century version of container-growing, using
open-weave osier baskets instead of the chilly black plastic
which we find wrapped round the roots of our modern nursery
trees or plants. The osier branches that the baskets were made of
were scalded first, to prevent them taking root themselves.

Layering

This is also a good time to make layers; that is to say, to make
roots sprout from low-growing branches, or from branches that
are pliable enough to be bent down into the ground while still
attached to the tree. The gardener cuts a notch in the branch
before burying it, to encourage it. He keeps the notch open with
a stick, small stone or piece of potsherd.

  To grow a vine in a pot a branch of the parent vine is
layered in spring, the layer being inserted through a pot. In the
autumn, when the vine is 'in full bearing' the shoot is cut off
below the pot and the plant taken to table; *a growing tree covered
in ripe fruit.* (Cobbett, 1833)

The garden paths

Grass paths are damp in Winter. Cobbett recommends gravel.
Grass is very bad; the traffic of muddy boots and heavily laden

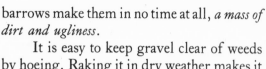

barrows make them in no time at all, *a mass of dirt and ugliness.*

It is easy to keep gravel clear of weeds by hoeing. Raking it in dry weather makes it neat and clean. An older gardener (William Forsyth, 1806) liked paths of sea-coal ashes. Slugs avoid them, *especially when new-laid and rough*; such walks also, *in some degree obstruct the passage of slugs and snails from one quarter to another.*

Edgings for the paths

Besides looking decorative, the edgings to paths have to be robust enough to stop the earth in the borders spilling on to the gravel. Large stones, glazed ornamental tiles, slates or bricks are one answer, but low-growing plants look prettier. Herbs are the obvious edging plants for a kitchen garden path. Evelyn liked chervil, which is an odd choice as it is rather delicate. Parsley, strawberries, violets, pinks and gillie flowers were also liked in Restoration gardens, though thyme, veronica, lavender, hyssop and rue were probably grown more often as they are shrubbier.

The Edwardians and Victorians liked flowery edgings such as thrift, double daisies and London pride as well as strawberries, but Cobbett condemned them; *all these herbaceous things ramble very quickly over the ground; extend their creepers over the walk, as well as over the adjoining ground; and, instead of being content to occupy the space of three inches wide they encroach to the extent of a foot the first summer; and, if left alone for only a couple of years, they will cover the whole of a walk six feet wide, harbouring all sorts of reptiles, making the walk pretty nearly as dirty as if it did not consist of gravel.* Cobbett is well known as an ardent political reformer, but like so many of the other writers who achieved eminence in different fields and are quoted in this book, he also had a passion for gardening. Observations like the one above should leave readers of *The English Gardener* in no doubt as to Cobbett's gardening expertise; in his youth he had worked as a garden boy at Kew Palace. What he liked best for edging was the dwarf form of box. It had been a favourite plant for this purpose for *ages upon ages* – or at least since Elizabethan times, when it was used on its own or as a border in knot gardens. Evelyn liked it too, calling it a most beautiful and useful shrub. Cobbett described it as *the most efficient of all possible things, and the prettiest*; he liked the colour and shape of its leaf, its *docility as to height, width and shape; its thriving in all sorts of soils, and in all sorts of aspects; its freshness under the hottest sun, and its defiance of all shade and all drip*. Moreover it is easy to propagate, easy to grow, and lasts a life-time.

To prevent Box from smelling after it is clipped

Box has one disadvantage that Cobbett does not mention. This is the slightly 'catty' smell which is particularly pungent after it has been clipped; maybe he liked it, others were more critical of it. *Upon clipping it offends, with the strong scent it casts, those that walk near it* wrote Leonard Meager, in 1699. *To remedy it, take this as a secret; Put some hard lime-stones in fair water, such as will not dissolve, yet give the water a taste and tincture, and after they have stood in it three or four hours, water it with this water, and the scent and offensiveness will be taken away from it.*

Odd jobs

Keep out extreme frosts from the fruit cellar, look over the onions and other dried roots. (1830)
    Renew the edgings of borders with herbs; mint, balm, sorrel, pennyroyal, tansy, tarragon, fennel

and burnet can all be planted from off-sets. (1830) Raggedy old box-borders can be revived by digging up the shrubs and replanting them more deeply in the ground. (1983)

Form and repair your gravel walks. (1830)

March weather is often tem-
perate, and sometimes warm. . . yet
the winds that usually blow from the Nor-
thern and Eastern regions, with the coldness of the Earth,
do so refrigerate the air, that it is not safe to remove your tender
plants, nor sow the seeds of tender Herbs. . . least the nipping Frosts
or winds, and sometimes snows, deprive you of your expectation.
(Worlidge, 1688) Nevertheless, there is a *multiplicity of business*
and in the warmer parts of the country, like a bather taking his
first swim of the year, the gardener gradually gains confidence
and removes protective mattings and other coverings from his
frost-tender plants and trees. As Switzer says: *Nature begins to be*
visibly warm and active, so also all good gardiners should with new
application and fresh vigour bestir themselves in all parts of their
gardens. . . if the extent of the garden be pretty large, and the
number of labourers proportionable, you may with pleasure, at one
cast of your eye, see them digging, making up, sowing, raking,
planting, howing, weeding etc . . . Before this month is out there
should be scarce a square or bed in the garden but what should be
either sown or planted. . . Neatness and politure ought now
particularly to glitter everywhere, and serve for a varnish to the
alleys and the dress'd grounds. (1727)

In the first week. . . . . the earthworm, and the snail and the
slug engender. . . . In the second week the Jackdaw begins to come to
Churches. . . . In the third week the turkey-cock struts and gobbles.
In the fourth week . . . field crickets open their holes and the

common flea appears. (Loudon's *Encyclopaedia*, 1822 edn)

March 23 1766. *Snow with thick ice, and a severe North-Wind.* March 24. *More snow, and fierce frost. Covered the fruit trees against the wall with boards and mats during these frosty nights. . . The fruit trees against the wall are much blown-out and in danger from this severe weather.* For the next three days it snowed heavily. The hot-beds were kept covered all day *but the plants lived in darkness.* The boards and mats were left on the wall-trees. March 28. *The snow melted in part. . . but it is still as deep as a horse's belly in many places.* By April 1 it had all gone. (From Gilbert White's *Garden Kalendar*)

Melon seeds

There are two ways to be sure of germination. One: when the melon is first cut, put it in a bowl of water. If it floats the seed is worthless, if it sinks, the seed will be good. (1858). Two: keep the seed in a warm place for a time before you sow it. Gilbert White wrote a memo on March 15 1755; *carry'd Mr Garnier's Canteleupe – seed (being but two years old) in my breeches pocket 6 or 8 weeks.*

The first pineapple in England

There are several versions of a painting of John Rose, gardener to Charles II, presenting his sovereign with a pineapple some time after 1668. The implication is that Rose grew it, but it's more likely that he only ripened the fruit which was already growing on a plant brought to him. The credit for being the first man to grow the pineapple in England goes to Mr Henry Telende, gardener to Sir Matthew Decker, a Dutch merchant living at Richmond, Surrey. The date is given as 1714. Few people had ever tasted the pineapple (which was a native of both the East and West Indies) but those who did thought it was marvellous. The Dutch connection helped Decker and his gardener; in Holland, at Amsterdam, they had hundreds of pineapples growing, but none with fruit.

Bees

The best kitchen gardens have always had beehives in them, and bee-keeping, like the care of the pigeon house and the ice house, the rabbit pens and the fish ponds, was all part of the gardener's job. Apart from providing quantities of honey and wax, the bee is a first-class pollinator of fruit. For this reason beehives were normally situated as close to the orchard or wall-trees as

possible, or even half in and half out of the fruit houses themselves. Many old garden walls have square cavities for the skeps to be placed in (see Packwood House in Warwickshire and the Memorial Garden at Canterbury Cathedral, or page 12 of Beatrix Potter's *Jemima Puddleduck*, 1908). Or there may be hedges with scoops cut out to shelter beehives, as at Erdigg, near Wrexham.

On a more commercial scale, professional bee-keepers in the New Forest hire out their hives, fully colonised, to the fruit growers of Kent, in March, April and May, for pollinating the blossom; while in China, whole trainloads of nomadic bee-keepers move northwards throughout the Spring.

Planting fruit trees

There is an old English dictum concerning apples, pears and other trees: *if you set them at All-Hallows-Tide, you may command them to prosper; but if after Candlemas, you must entreat them to grow.* However Gilbert White left the planting of his new pear trees till March 1st. He planted the following kinds in the following groups: Chaumontelle; Virgoleuse; Crasane, Doyenné; St Germain; Brown Bury (Beurré); Doyenné; Autumn Burgamot and Swan's Egg. It appears that these were espaliers, planted along the alleys of the quarters of his new garden. In May of the year before (1761) he had begun building a great fruit wall for the new garden; it was finished in late June. On December 30th he planted thirteen trees; every other one was a vine, which suggests that they were allowed to arch over the peaches and nectarines like those illustrated by Samuel Collins in his *Paradise Retrieved* of 1717. There was a passion flower at each end of the wall, five vines, three nectarines, two peaches and an apricot. This was the arrangement:

| Passion Flower | Breda Apricot | Sweetwater Vine | Roman Nectarine | Murdoch Middleton's Sweetwater Vine | Nobless Peach | Mr Snooke's Black Cluster Vine |

| Roman Nectarine | Mr Snooke's White Muscadine Vine | Nobless Peach | John Hale's White Muscadine Vine | Newington Nectarine | Passion Flower |

White records their growth and his care for them for several years to come, he covers their roots with straw in a heavy February frost; *cuts them down* in the following March, (by which he means either heading them down or pruning); disbuds them in April; tacks and disbuds the vines in May; washes leaves two or three times a week during a burning June; gathers his first sweetwater and black cluster grapes in the September of 1764; trims and tacks all the trees and vines again in November and digs the border. In September 1765, four years after planting he rather disconsolately gathers his only nectarine, it was not ripe, but the earwigs had been at it, so that it couldn't come to anything. He also gathered his first peach, *tender, white and juicy*, . . . but not so highly flavoured as some he has met with; he describes his white grapes as *very eatable but not highly flavoured*; the apricot finally produces a *decent crop* in 1766.

The origins of the potato

The herbalist Gerard is responsible for a mistake about the origins of the potato that has lasted 300 years. He had a garden in Holborn, just behind what is now the Patent Office. In his *Herbal* of 1597 he illustrates, names and describes the potato which he was growing there (and was then a complete rarity) as a native of Virginia (*Battata Virginiana*). It was not until the 20th century that the potato was declared to be quite definitely indigenous to South America. During the late 1580s, English privateers, among them Sir Francis Drake and Sir Walter Raleigh, had doubtless come across potatoes in raids on Spanish ships and in West Indian or South American Spanish colonies such as Hispaniola and Cartagena where they were cultivated for food. Gerard's mistake was possibly caused by potatoes taken from Spanish ships getting mixed up with samples of plants from the North American colonies.

Although Raleigh never went to Virginia he is said to be the first to grow the potato in Ireland (in 1587) where he had an estate. The legend here is that his gardener thought that the little green apple-like fruits formed by the flowers were the part to be eaten (he was not alone in making this mistake). Imagine his surprise when, on being ordered to 'weed them out' the poor fellow found bushels and bushels of 'Virginian' potatoes hanging to the roots.

Potato varieties

In 1629 three different vegetables were known as 'potatoes'. Parkinson listed the 'Virginian potato', the 'Canadian potato'

(Jerusalem artichoke) and the 'Spanish potato', which was the original 'battata', known today as the sweet potato. In 1664 the potato as we know it was either 'Virginian', which had purple flowers, or 'Irish' which had white. In 1728 there were four varieties, the kidney, the white, the Lancashire (which was pink) and the red, which had a rough coat. (Poor men ate white potatoes, rich men ate red.) Fifty years later there were still the same four kinds; the early red, called the wife's potato, the large round dark red, the round white and the white kidney. By the beginning of Queen Victoria's reign different sorts of potato were 'as numerous as the stones of the pavement of a large city', though few of them were mentioned in gardening books by name. By the end of the nineteenth century, Robinson in his great vegetable book *The Vegetable Garden* declares that there must be many thousands of different varieties of potato, and limits himself to describing fifty. The gardenless potato eater must wonder though at the meagre lack of choice in the greengrocer's. 'Red, white or Edwards', is all there is today, which gives us about as much choice as there was in 1664.

Potatoes, parsley and Good Friday

Good Friday is the traditional day for planting potatoes in England (among amateurs this is, professional gardeners get the day off). In Ireland they do this on the day of their Patron Saint, Patrick, which is March 17th. As Good Friday can never be before March 21st, but can fall a full month later, the exact date for potato planting clearly doesn't matter.

Good Friday is also supposed to be the best day to sow parsley, as it is of all plants the one most affected by the Devil. As everyone knows, Good Friday is the one day on which the Devil is powerless.

Companion planting for potatoes

Plant marigolds near potatoes to keep off eelworms. Plant early peas between the rows to shelter young potato shoots. Plant foxgloves to improve the storage life of clamped potatoes.

Pliny's pelleted seeds

Pliny says he *found this stated in a poem*. He doesn't say who wrote it, nor does it seem as though he actually tried it for himself, but here is the recipe. It's interesting, if only as an indication that there's nothing new about pelleted seeds. *If pellets of goat's dung, the size of a bean, are hollowed out, and the seed of leeks, rocket, lettuces, parsley, endive and cresses is inserted in them, and then sown, the plants will thrive in a marvellous degree.* Pliny died in A.D. 79.

Odd jobs

Cut strips of Rosemary as soon as it flowers, which is commonly this month. (1691) *Mingle clay or over-moist soil plentifully with brick-dust.* (1691) *Bring in materials for the Birds in the Aviary to build their nests withal.* (1691) *Take care not to leave open the door of the fruit cellar; its temperature must remain below 40°F.* (1823) *Stick branches of Fern, Fir or Yew amongst Apricot, Nectarine and Peach trees on walls, or hang mats or old fishing nets before them, to defend them from hail.* (1729)

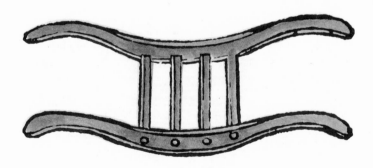

In this Month your Garden

appears in its greatest Beauty, the

Blossoms of the Fruit-trees prognosticate

the plenty of Fruits for all the succeeding Summer-
Months, unless prevented by untimely Frosts or Blights. The bees
now buz in every Corner . . . to seek for Food: the Birds sing in
every Bush and the sweet Nightingale tunes her warbling Notes in
your solitary Walks, whilst the other Birds are at their rest. The
Beasts of the Woods look out into the Plains; And the Fishes of the
Deep sport themselves in the shallow Waters. The Air is wholesome,
and the Earth pleasant, beginning now to be clothed with Nature's
best Array, exceeding all Art's Glory. (Worlidge, 1688)

    *This is the Month for very unsettled weather, sometimes warm
and kindly, with frequent but gentle showers of Rain, at other times
the nights are frosty, with a continu'd dry Easterly Wind which is
very harmful to the Fruit and Kitchen Garden.* (Miller, 1731)

    *April 5. 1757. Unusual hot weather this week; during which,
John, who was but a very young Gardener, scorched up, and
suffocated all his forward Cucumbers: and drawed his melon-plants
in the pots but has not spoiled them.*

    *April 21. 1757. Snowed very hard for sixteen hours: the
greatest snow that has fallen this year; and must have been a foot deep
had it not for the greatest part melted as it fell. Went away without
any frost, and seems to have done no damage.*

    *April 13. 1759. . . . a perfect summer's day, that fetched ye
beds* [hot-beds] *finely to their heat after such gluts of rain. Saw*

seven swallows, the first this year, playing about James Knight's House. (Gilbert White)

Blanched seakale and rhubarb

This is the season for seakale and rhubarb from the open garden. By now the weather will have been warm enough for them to be well grown, delicately flavoured, tender, succulent and pale, thanks to the upturned pots, large covered drain pipes, chimney pots, barrels, tubs, boxes or old buckets that have been shielding the growing plants from the extremes of cold and the least glimmer of light, ever since New Year's Day.

Special earthenware pots were made for blanching. The earliest seakale pots appeared about 1822. Some were domed and had a handle on top like tall meat covers, but the best had moveable lids, so that the gardener could inspect and cut his crop without disturbing the plant, or the dung linings surrounding the pot.

A gentleman's gardener was expected to supply his master with a constant succession of seakale or rhubarb from Christmas

to Whitsun. This was done by starting to force roots indoors
over heat, in October or as soon as the plant became dormant
after the first frosts. The forced shoots would continue till late
March when the outdoor plants took over. Without forcing,
both the seakale and rhubarb season are very brief.

Seakale

Special seakale forcing-pots were patented and manufactured
for indoor forcing in the late nineteenth and early twentieth
century when seakale was at the height of its popularity,
especially among the well-to-do classes. Today it is regarded as
either an unobtainable luxury, or else a curiosity, yet it is one of
the easiest plants to grow, one of the most delicious vegetables to
eat and is moreover, a native of our own seashores. The first
mention of it as a garden vegetable is by Philip Miller, in his
Gardener's Dictionary of 1731. He noted that gentlemen with
gardens near the sea, in Devon, grew it but gave no instruction
as to blanching it. Gilbert White on April 6th, 1751 wrote that
he had obtained some 'sea-cale' seed from *the South-hams of
Devon* and had sown a large bed of it. He noted that it took at
least six weeks to germinate, mentions weeding it in the March
of next year, but thereafter he never mentions it again. The
Quaker botanist and physician John Lettsom was more
successful. He grew it in his extensive garden at Grove Hill,
Camberwell where he lived from 1779. But the greatest
champion of seakale was one of Lettsom's friends, another
Quaker, the Hampshire-born botanist and apothecary William
Curtis (founder of the *Botanical Magazine*). In 1830
J. C. Loudon says *it is now a common vegetable in Covent Garden
Market and has even begun to appear on the green-stalls of the
Scottish metropolis.*

Rhubarb

Like seakale, rhubarb is almost unknown on the Continent,
though it is eaten in North America. Like seakale too its history

[66]

in the kitchen garden is comparatively recent, though the roots have been used medicinally for centuries.

The plant is a native of China, where its cultivation is ancient. It is also indigenous to Northern India, Tibet, Mongolia, the Volga basin, Siberia, Persia and Turkey. The name is said to be a combination of 'Rha', which is the ancient name of the River Volga and 'Barbarum' or Tartary, from whence it came.

Quantities of the dried root of Chinese rhubarb (*Rheum Rhaponticum*) were imported by the apothecaries for use as a purgative and tonic, but it was not grown here to any large extent, except by apothecaries, until the mid-18th century. Parkinson claims to be the first person to grow the true 'Rhubarbe' in England, in 1629. He calls it *Rhaponticum verum,* and describes it as a *kind of round leaved Dock* with *goodly large leaves,* a stalk *of the bignesse of any man's thumbe,* two feet long or more, with *whitish flowers, contrary to all other Dockes.* His woodcut shows that it is indeed 'true rhubarb', so it is rather worrying to find that he also recommends cooking the leaves in a syrup. *The leaves have a fine acid taste* and *cannot but be very effectuall in dejected appetites and hot fits of agues.*

There is no mention in England of eating the stems until 1739, when Peter Collinson wrote in a letter to his friend John Bartram that he was sending him some Siberian rhubarb seed.

He wanted him to try growing it in America. This was the *Rheum undulatum* with curled or wavy leaves. It had been given him by the Professor of Botany at Petersburg, who may also have supplied the recipe for rhubarb pie. *All you have to do, is to take the stalks from the root and from the leaves; peel off the rind and cut them in two or three pieces, and put them in crust with sugar and a little cinnamon; then bake the pie, or tart; eats best cold. . .*

Eventually, around 1810, a hybrid variety and a cross between *R. Rhaponticum* and *R. undulatum* became our culinary rhubarb. In 1817 it was accidentally discovered (by Knight, at Chelsea) that rhubarb could be forced and blanched like seakale. This greatly improved its taste and succulence, and thus its popularity.

In the meantime, such was the expense of importing the roots of the medicinal variety (some £200,000 per annum in 1770) that the London Society of Arts offered gold medals to anyone who could grow more than 100 plants. It was probably the concentration on the more financially rewarding medicinal variety that delayed the development of the culinary kind. Even as late as 1865, when the plant was quite extensively grown in market gardens it was being described as *no unworthy substitute for fruit in spring tarts*; it was regarded as rather an odd sort of vegetable, rather than as a fruit in its own right.

Oranges and orangeries

In April 1691, the owners of orange trees were advised (by Evelyn) that *If the weather prove benign*, they may adventure about the middle of this month to bring their orange trees out of the conservatory; *let it be only in a fair day, giving a refreshment of water not too cold*. By the time Charles II was King, the passion for oranges and for the trees themselves, as garden ornaments was at its height. The first trees were being grown here a hundred years before Charles II ascended the throne. Sir Francis Carew, a keen gardener and a courtier to Queen Elizabeth, was said to be the first person to have been given

orange-tree seeds in 1585 (by Walter Raleigh); he was the first to grow the trees in English soil, and the first to obtain fully grown trees from the Continent in 1592.

The wise Mulberry tree

Gentlemen who wished to know *the best and securest season* for exposing their orange trees and more tender curiosities were advised (by Evelyn) to observe the Mulberry tree. *When it*

begins to put forth and open the leaves (be it earlier or late) bring your oranges etc boldly out of the Conservatory. This advice is very sound. Old gardeners still call the Mulberry *the Wise Tree*, because it never shows a leaf until all danger of frost is past.

Skirrets

The reputation of the Skirret as an aphrodisiac has not done much for its survival. Most people have never heard of it today; few of those that do know of it have either eaten or grown it, yet from Roman times and up until the mid-nineteenth century it was extremely popular. It is probably Chinese in origin, and owes its English name to a corruption of the Danish *Sokerot*, which is indicative of its chief characteristic which is that it is, for a vegetable, incredibly sweet. It is also white and rather mushy when cooked. It can be sown either from seed, or planted as sets taken from last year's crop. Start it off in April, and it is ready to eat in September. The nearest thing to it in flavour is a parsnip. To cook it you boil the roots before peeling them, then mash them up with butter.

Hot-beds

A hot-bed is one of the oldest and most satisfactory methods of producing early salads, or vegetables, or fruits, or flowers. It generates constant and gentle heat. Shade and protection from the outside elements is provided by window-like sashes; the heat is created by a heap of fermenting dung which, by careful management, can be kept at a temperature of between 60° and 80°F for several weeks. The first mention of a hot-bed is to be found in one of the earliest garden books ever printed – Didymus Mountain's *Gardener's Labyrinth* of 1577. He suggests making one *to hasten the fruits  forward of mellons*. John Gerard, in his *Herbal* of 1597, recommends making *in mid-Aprill or sooner. . . a bank or bed of hot and new horse dung taken forth from the stable (and not from the dunghill) an ell* [45 inches] *in breadth and the like in depth or thickness, of what length you please, according to the quantitie of seed*. This was in order to grow cucumbers. The bed was covered with *the most fertillest earth finely sifted, to a depth of six* *inches*; the seeds were sown, the bed was covered with straw and after a week watered (with warm water, to avoid checking the seedling's growth or cooling the bed). Hoops and poles were arranged as props for the straw mats or *old painted cloths* that were to protect the plants from cold; a slight improvement on the *boards or tables set on pillars or other stayes of stone* suggested in the *Gardener's Labyrinth*. Either way, whatever the covers, the beds had to be closed *everie night. . . and opened when the daie is warmed with sun beames*.

By the time of the Restoration the hot-bed was being brought into use long before Christmas, *it affords us (in Winter) all the novelties of the Spring*. This is Jean de la Quintinie, the Royal French Gardener. At Versailles he grew in winter, cucumbers, melons, radishes, small salads, 'greens', flowers and asparagus. One of his admirers was John Evelyn and as a result of their friendship much that was done in the great French gardens of that time was copied in England.

Hot-beds may still be of use. In the late 1940s when a gentleman's gardener, recently de-mobbed, was faced with the task of supplying the household with early forced fruit and vegetables as in pre-war times, he found the boilers gone for scrap; even if they had been spared the fuel for them was rationed and the greenhouses had been blasted empty of glass. Hot-beds solved the problem.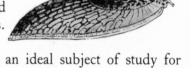

The hot-bed is of course an ideal subject of study for students of alternative technology, as long as they drive horses rather than motor cars.

Odd jobs

This is the best month for building roads, paths, drains, walls (after the danger of frost is over) and fences. (1830)

Sweep and clean alleys. Cover blossoming Peach trees with pea-haulms, leave them on till the fruit is the size of your little finger. Do the same for Apricots and wall-plums. (1706)

Gather up worms and snails after evening showers. Make soot-ashes and the sweepings of tobacco stalks into a fine dust, strew it half an inch thick at the foot of trees, to prevent Pismires [ants] *and other crawling insects from invading the Fruit. Weed and Haugh betimes. Open now your Bee-hives, for now they hatch. Look carefully to them and prepare your Hives, etc.* (1691)

The Titlark sings; the cuckoo is heard; the gudgeon spawns . . . black snails abound and the large bat appears. (1830) *Though there be often very warm days in this month, yet there are often cold nights . . . cover the hot-beds with mats each evening about six or seven o'clock, and take them off next morning at six or seven o'clock.* (1779)

May is sometimes very hot and dry, which greatly retards the growth of most vegetables, and at other times it is cold and moist, whereby the markets are greatly stocked with most kinds of esculent plants. But as this occasions plenty of most sorts of plants, so it also increases the numbers and sizes of weeds . . . no time should be lost (in eradicating them) in such a season. (Philip Miller, 1731)

He that delights not in Physick, let him now exercise himself in the Garden, and take the Smell of the Earth, with the rising Sun, than which to the vertuously inclined there is nothing more pleasant; for now is Nature full of Mirth, and the Senses stored with Delights, and variety of Pleasures. (1688)

Vegetables and fruit in season

Coleworts and other herbes, (being eaten with contentment are better than a fatted ox without it), sage (with butter), leeks, parsley, thyme, marjoram, sorrell, spinage etc. Scorzonera, asparagus, lettice, purslain . . . early cherries, strawberries near the end [of the month]. (*The Scots Gard'ner*, 1683)

There is now no longer occasion to demand why such and such spots of ground are yet bare; because you are now going to be supply'd with colly flowers, cardons, sellery, cabbage lettuces, and even artichokes too, which could not appear more early; and now also purslain comes in great plenty by nature to gild the earth, and offers itself in abundance to pleasure its master; green pease are like to satisfie the longing appetite of the dainty pallate in abundance; and mushrooms shoot up in abundance. (Switzer, 1727)

Purslane

The 'gilding of the earth' by purslane is a sight not often met with in today's kitchen gardens, but it was a favourite salad ingredient in the eighteenth and early nineteenth centuries. There are two kinds; the yellow-leaved or golden variety so much admired by Switzer (*Portulaca sativa*) and the hardier green-leaved sort (*Portulaca oleracea*). To have it in May, it was sown on a hot-bed, with other small salletings, but it will grow in English gardens out of doors in a warm, sunny spot if sown from April onwards. It is a favourite salad with Indian, Middle Eastern and Greek people who call it *glistirida*.

Women gardeners

Women were welcome additions to the lower echelons of the kitchen garden workforce when there was more than usual to do. Apart from the traditional task of weeding the beds and paths, women (and children) were paid for gathering insects, snails, slugs and worms and occasionally, for picking fruit. Needless to say a woman's wages were less than half a man's for the same hours of work; 6 shillings for a six-day week when a labourer in the same garden earned 16/6d in 1823; but there were perks. 'A. Teisel', Loudon's invented woman gardener is reported to be *much pleased with her Epinal hat, and also with the Swiss working dress given her by my Lady Almeria*. This entry, in Loudon's fictitious time-book, was made after Mrs Loudon became the editor, in 1850.

Weeding

From now until the weather becomes cooler, weeding is a constant chore. William Lawson wrote in 1621 that *the skill and paine of weeding the garden with weeding knives or fingers* should be referred to ladies, housewives and their maids. *Take the opportunitie after a showre of raine, withall I advise the mistresse either be present herself, or teach her maids to know hearbs from weeds.*

[76]

John Reid recognised weeding as *the most material part of gard'nery* and suggested: *in beds where hawes cannot go, you must weed with your hands on both sides, sitting in a furrow on a straw cushion . . . taking the help of a weeding iron . . . as soon as you perceive a weed peep, you may chalk it.* (1683)

Asparagus

Asparagus has occupied a large portion of the grander kitchen gardens for the last 300 years. It still does, where anyone has enough space to grow it. *The asparaginous class of esculents may be considered as . . . one of luxury,* wrote Loudon, who reckoned that it could take up as much as one-eighth of a gentleman's garden, *but it does not enter in to that of the cottager.* Compared to the Continent, English aspar- agus growing in the 16th century was on a very small scale, but in the 17th century Dutch asparagus began to appear in our gardens. This, as described by Parkinson, in 1629, *is of much greater account, because the stalks are larger, whiter, and being dressed, taste more sweet and pleasant.* The English asparagus was thin and

green. It was probably introduced by the Romans who had a passion for asparagus. It grew wild in various parts of the country, notably near Bristol and can occasionally be found, growing wild in the extreme west. It looks as if both white and green kinds were grown at Longleat; in 1680 Lady Frances Thynne in a letter to her husband Thomas, wrote: *I had a fine dish of asparagus last night for supper, some of them large ones;*

which I thought was a rairity, but I cannot tell whether it is or no.

Switzer reports, in 1724 *There are some who dress their beds with the dung of pigeons or poultry which by reason of its great salaciousness, heats and enriches the ground below to a very great degree, and will then produce stalks of an uncommon dimension, and cause a hundred of the grass to weigh from twenty to twenty five pounds or more*, (this would mean a pound bundle had only four or five stalks in it. Is he exaggerating? Pliny says the Romans grew it so large, at Ravenna, that three stalks would make up a pound). But to return to Switzer; *I must leave it to the disquisition of curious palates, and to experience whether grass so large, and which is dunged with such a nasty dung, can be good, or indeed any better than those which are rais'd at or about Lambeth.*

Asparagus is also called *coralwort*, because of its red berries, and *sparrowgrass*, because, according to Batty Langley, the first shoots resemble a sparrow's bill.

The advice in 1727 on how to cook and serve asparagus can be followed today. *Do not let them abide long in water after they are boil'd, but as soon as ever the boiling is over, the putting them unstringed or untied, on the backside of a plate, there to be drain'd of all its moisture, and then sprinkled with salt, and butter'd is, in the opinion of some very curious gentlemen, of great value.* (1727)

Advice to the young gardener

The human animal, in common with most other indigenous to our climate, is generally in high spirits and vigour during this month. Woe to the young gardener who exhausts his spirits in any way other than self-improvement. (Loudon, 1830 edn)

Protecting fruit blossom from frost

Blossom time is nerve-racking for the fruit grower. Lustful in their desire for what were originally Middle Eastern fruits such as the peach, the apricot and the nectarine, yet conscious of the risk of losing them and whole crops of early-flowering apples,

cherries, pears or plums because of a late, sneaky British frost, gardeners to the gentry have for centuries tried out various ways to protect their fruit trees during these crucial weeks. The most dangerous period is often during 'the days of the Icy Saints'; these fall in the first or second weeks of May – depending on whether you go by the new or old calendar. R D Blackmore is well known as the author of *Lorna Doone*, but less well known as

a fruit grower and author of *Kit and Kitty*, a three-volume blood and thunder novel set in a fruit garden in Sunbury, Middlesex. In this book he describes the situation from first-hand experience; *The bloom of England hovers in nightly peril, from the middle of April to the very end of May. It is one of the many sad things we meet, but can only fold our hands and watch, that for nearly six weeks of the year, and in early seasons even more. . . the fruit crop trembles on the hazard of a single night's caprice. The bright sun and the lovely day delude the folk who know no better; these are the very things that lead to the starry night, and the quiet cold, and the white sheet over the grass at five a.m., and the black death following.* (1890)

An eighteenth-century notion for protecting blossom from frost was to use long bands of straw and hemp. These, like the laggings on water pipes were wound round the stem of the tree and along the principal branches; the ends hung down into a vessel of water and were kept in place by a stone. The frost was supposed to *operate on the water*. It acted like a lightning conductor, presumably.

Glass and other copings

For most of the 18th century, and well into the 19th, the problem of how to protect wall-fruit blossom from late frosts was solved either by using netting, or by the use of boards laid like shelves along the walls as recommended by Miller and

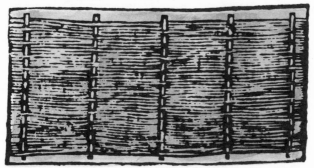

Switzer. By 1830 these 'temporary copings' had become quite ingenious. Two planks laid side by side and joined made a projection of about 18″ wide. They were attached to hinges which fitted into 'irons' at the top of the wall. By means of pulleys these could be raised or lowered like a visor over the fruit trees. When not projecting from the top of the wall they were laid flat on top of the coping. Later still, in 1884, *The*

Gardener's Chronicle advertised a projecting coping made of iron and glass. They came in *various widths, from a foot to a yard according to the height of the wall.* . . . their advantage over boards was that they admitted light and could be removed in the summer *when the night dews are beneficial to the foliage of the trees.*

Odd jobs

Thin out the apricot fruit, pinch pear tree shoots and don't let peach or pear boughs grow between wall and trellis. Weed and hoe. (1727)

Destroy caterpillars. Stick peas, if the rows run east-west, on the southern side, so that as they lean towards the sun they will catch hold more easily. (1706)

Set your bees at full liberty, look out often, and expect swarms. (1691)

Continue to protect your tender plants, nightly. (1830)

. . . *The beans were deliciously sweet-scented and* [had] *a white flower something like Whitsuntide stock.* At *the Lower House the orchard boughs were so thick and close that the sun could not penetrate them, and the sunlight only got into the orchard at a gap in the west side through which it came streaming in a long bright streak along the brilliant green rich velvety-looking grass like sunshine through a painted Cathedral window. Sitting room windows open till very late* . . . (Kilvert's *Diary* Friday, 3 June, 1870)

The days at longest, the mornings and evenings the most pleasant times for Recreation . . . *the plenty of cooling Fruits and Tillage now furnish your Table, and tempt the curious Pallate to exchange a great part of its grosser food for garden dainties.* . . (1688)

A taste of things to come

The bedded musk melons, the forward Apricots and some little muscat-pears upon wall-trees, endeavour to show us by some little samples, the riches which they altogether promise us in greater Abundance in the month next immediately ensuing. . . (Evelyn's translation of la Quintinie, 1693)

Bothy life and the journeyman-gardener

Qualified gardeners were usually at least 20 years old, having served their time as boys, apprentices and labourers. If they were single they could apply for 'bothy and full attendance' as part of their wages. (Between the First and Second World Wars a journeyman's wage was about 30 shillings (£1.50p) a week; 8/6d (42½p) went on food; cigarettes were 10½d (4p) for 20; beer 5d (2½p) a pint.)

The bothy, if they were lucky, was a proper cottage; but often it was no more than a series of small, dark, poky rooms among the sheds behind the greenhouses. Loudon's ideal bothy was well-equipped, with a water-pump and drain in the outer lobby; a living room or kitchen furnished with a proper range and boiler; a bedroom above, *where the bedsteads should be of iron, narrow and curtainless for not more than one person.* There should also be clothes cupboards.

The gardeners' work began at 6 a.m. The garden boys cooked their breakfast for them at 8. The village shop delivered most of their necessities; vegetables came from their own employer's garden and the meat supply could be augmented by 'arrangements' with the gamekeeper. In summertime the dairymaid would be wheedled into giving them fresh cream, in exchange for peaches.

The duties of a garden boy

Roy Shadbolt was 15 in 1950 and a garden boy at Cornbury Park at Charlbury in Oxfordshire. The owners were then the Watneys, of brewing fame. His wages for a 5½-day week were £2 2s 6d. He lived at home. He left home at 7.15 a.m. and cycled to the Park. He picked up the list of what was wanted each day from the cook at the house on his way to the kitchen gardens. Back in the gardens the day followed whatever routine the head gardener planned. One of the traditional duties for the garden boys at Cornbury was in the greenhouses, pollinating whatever needed it, by means of a rabbit tail attached to a stick. Another was to sweep all the paths and the steps leading to the gardener's house every Saturday morning at 11.30 a.m. sharp, to leave it spotless for the weekend.

The cook

Mrs Newstead, now 90, was the cook at Pylewell Park, near Lymington in Hampshire from 1921-1939. She never had to buy anything from a greengrocer's shop, except oranges and lemons. She was catering for a minimum of 25 people in the house and everything came from the gardens. With produce

from the home farm, game from the estate and fish from local fishermen (the estate is bounded on one side by the Solent) the only shop she had anything to do with was the town's best grocer Rowland Hill's (now Woolworth's).

She had three or four helpers in the kitchen: a head kitchen maid, a second kitchen maid and one or two scullery maids. The rest of the household was composed of: seven 'family'; a French governess, a nanny, a nursery maid; two or three ladies' maids; the butler, two footmen, a hall boy; five housemaids and the odd-job man. Meals of varying degrees of grandness were served simultaneously in four different places – in the nursery, the dining room, the servants hall and in Mrs Newstead's own sitting room. Mrs Newstead had complete confidence in Mr Hamilton, the head gardener. I think this is because she was quite terrifying to work for, at all events she says *he always had what was wanted.*

Peas on the fourth of June

Where gardening is carried on upon a royal, or almost royal scale, peas are raised by means of artificial heat, in order to have them

here at the same time that they have them in Portugal, which is in the months of December and January. Beneath this royal state however, the next thing is to have them in the natural ground as early as possible; and that may sometimes be by the middle of May, and hardly ever later than the first week of June. This was the situation as described by Cobbett, in 1833. He adds: *The late King, George III, reigned so long (1760-1820) that his birthday formed a sort of season with gardeners; and ever since I became a man, I can recollect that it was always deemed a sign of bad gardening if there were not green peas in the garden fit to gather on the fourth of June.* To do this, peas of an early kind had to be sown in November in as sunny and sheltered a spot as possible, usually against a south wall; they were protected from winter frosts by covers of old pea-haulms and straw.

Ways to destroy insects and other pests in Summer

Children can be quite useful in this respect, though most gardening books recommend employing boys rather than girls. Boys, by playing football, will frighten away *Moles* and *boys will discover wasps' nests in the day time and at night. When all the*

enemy are encamped, fire the train [of gunpowder] *and their destruction follows in a few seconds, not one of them escaping.* (1828) Or they can drop oil on wasps' backs, which is fatal as *it closes up the pores through which they breathe. Earwigs and wood-lice* are to be found hiding in hollow places. A very old trick is *to put sheep's hooves on sticks. . . they'll creep in in the morning to hide by day and are then easy to catch and kill.* Where they attack currants, peaches and nectarines, cut broad-bean stems, or the hollow stems of Jerusalem artichokes or sunflowers, about five or six inches long; *there is a sweetness in the inside which attracts them, and they readily take shelter in them from rain.* Place bundles of these stems horizontally in the tree; examine them daily and blow the earwigs etc. out into scalding water. Or you could have bought Edward's Earwig Trap, made at Paul Square, Birmingham in 1858.

To catch ants, make a smooth hole in the ground, they will fall in and can't get out, you can then drown them; or put

saucers of oil with sugar round the edge to tempt them. They will drown in the oil. (1828)

To kill *caterpillars* on gooseberry bushes (which they often render leafless at this time of year); water the bushes with a mixture of boiled elder leaves which will be quite black when cleared and cooled, to which is added an equal amount of tobacco water. In ten minutes the caterpillars will fall off. Tobacco water was made by pouring half a gallon of boiling water onto the strongest shag tobacco to be had. It was the best spray for getting rid of *black fly* and *grubs of all kinds*, on fruit trees. Tobacco smoke for fumigating the fruit houses, was made very simply by making small pieces of cast iron red-hot, putting them in large flower pots and covering the hot iron with as much tobacco as was necessary completely to fill the house with smoke. Fumigating bellows were being made by 1822, and as these were portable, trees outside could also be treated.

Slugs, snails and *worms* were either picked up by hand *at night in the summer with a candle as they creep out or early morning after raine.* Or treated to a lethal dose made of walnut leaves steeped in boiling water; this infusion was then mixed with lime water, soap-suds and urine. Peas, lettuces and strawberries were protected by a *cordon sanitaire* of slaked lime and wood ashes, which snails and slugs would not pass or, alternatively, they could be planted in beds bordered by slates or board-coping which had been coated with a mixture of train-oil and soot. Some of these old-fashioned remedies may seem repugnant to the modern gardener, but they do at least have the advantage of being both organic and cheap.

Gardeners and smoking

Tobacco (best strong shag) was strictly for use as a fumigant or spray; it must have been difficult to resist smoking it as well, but the rule in all gardens was firm. No one was allowed to smoke. In some places the head gardener, and only the head gardener, had permission. The reason was partly horticultural

REGISTERED JULY 2. 1877

discipline (tobacco is fatal to tomato plants, for example), partly for appearance's sake. Smoking was regarded as a pleasure; no man could look as if he was really working with a pipe or cigarette in his mouth. Needless to say, the rule was broken by die-hards, whenever they got the chance. The following exchange, related by an old gardener, reads like a caption from an Edwardian copy of *Punch*: Gardener, puffing at a pipe sees

Ladyship coming and stuffs it in his pocket. Ladyship 'Fred, you're smoking.' 'No, m'lady, I'm not.' 'You *are* smoking Fred.' 'No, my lady I am not.' 'Yes, you are, your pocket's on fire. . .'

Gardeners liked to play practical jokes on one another too. *We played a good trick one wet afternoon. There was an awful old gardener who always smoked a terrible pipe. We were all in a row working in the potting shed, breaking up dried stable dung with our hands for potting compost when Fred was called away. He left his pipe on the bench. We knocked out his tobacco and replaced it with a twist of tarred string and a lump of dried dung.* To their delight, when he came back he picked up his pipe and lit it, and smoked it, and *never said a word.*

Hampers to town

It seems perverse that just when the great kitchen gardens were in full swing, producing all the best fruits, salads and vegetables of early Summer, the family would pack up and decamp to London for two or three months, to enjoy 'the Season'. This began with the opening of the Royal Academy's Summer Show, in May. It continued with endless coming-out parties and balls throughout June (there was also Ascot) and ended at Henley with the Royal Regatta at the beginning of July. The family didn't necessarily return home then, but went racing at Goodwood at the end of July, or to Cowes for the first week in August. The whole family went to the seaside or Scotland (for the salmon and grouse) for the rest of the month and most of September. What happened to all the produce at home? None of it was wasted; all the fruit, flowers and vegetables followed the family to town, dispatched by the gardeners once or twice a week in huge hampers.

The artichoke

No vegetable has more attributions to its name than the artichoke, and none has more different spellings. To begin with its name, which is also a good way to chart the course of its history; most authorities state that 'artichoke' comes from the Arabic *al-kharshuf, al-karsufa, al-kharstif* or *al-harshaf*, meaning 'rough skinned'. The plant travelled from that country to Italy, where it became the *articiocco* or *alcarcioffo*. There the name was thought to derive from *arci* meaning arch, combined with *cioffo* meaning horse-collar or *ciocco* – stump. It went from Naples to France in 1466 and took the name of *artichaut*; to the French the obvious derivations were from *haut* or *hault* meaning high, and *chau* or *chou* meaning cabbage, as well as *chaud* meaning warm. At last, round about the time of King Henry VIII it came to England, and was known variously as hartichoak or artychoake or hartychock or  artichoke. Here, our own etymologists put the harty part of the name down to *hortus* (Latin for garden) while the choke with its tickly, thistly seed heads is so called because that is precisely what happens if you try to eat it. The OED lists over twenty ways of spelling it.

Paper lights and frames

The precursors to today's light, protective and transparent frames and cloches were made of nothing more than oiled paper or calico pasted over thin strips of wood. They were both transparent and waterproof, firm and light; they also protected melons or cucumbers on hot-beds against the extremes of cold and wet, light or heat, and they came into use from the beginning of June till the end of July.

Odd jobs

*Employ a few children to pick up caterpillars; pour hot water over
ants' nests or burn straw on them. (Tarred cord round a fruit-tree
prevents them climbing up it.) Employ a boy with a net to keep going
round the garden, catching butterflies and moths.* (1828)

*Box will want clipping, but do it in moist weather. Uncover
wall-fruits to the sun, especially Peaches. Clear useless fruit-tree
shoots and shorten some. Spread thin mats over the glasses of the
melon frames from* 11 *till* 2 *o'clock, also till the middle of the month,
cover them at night.* (1779)

Gather Herbs in the Full [sun] *to keep dry.* (1691)

*Begin to destroy Insects with Hoofs, Canes and tempting
Baits. Gather Snails after Rain. Look to your Bees for swarms and
casts; look to your Aviary, for now the Birds grow sick of their
Feathers, therefore assist them with Emulsions of the cooler seeds
bruised in their water, as melons, cucumbers, etc. Also give them
Succory, Beets, Groundsel, Chickweed, Fresh Gravel and Earth
etc.* (1691)

Net cherries, water strawberries. (1779)

Gather scorzonera seed, when the dew has gone. (1706)

July 7. The weather has been so perfectly hot, and bright for these five days past that my Hay was all cut

and made in that time . . . *June 21. Mr Cane's Cantaloupes were all burn-up, with a noble crop on them about ten days before the crop would have been ripe. He had a fine crop; but the intense heat scorched off all the fibres thro' his light, dusty earth. July 23. Unusual hot summer weath[er] for three weeks past. Wheat harvest is begun in some places. July 26. The hot vehement season continues: the ground is wonderfully burnt. July 31. Now a great rain after several months drought.* (Gilbert White, *Garden Kalendar*, 1759)

July 4. Soft, showery growing weather. July 9. Showery weather still. Putty'd the melon frames to keep out the wet. July 14. Showery weather. July 19. Very wet weather. July 29. A vast rain. The hay lies about in miserable heaps. (Gilbert White, *Garden Kalendar*, 1763)

That year it rained for five weeks fròm 29th June until 3rd August, and continued to do so for the rest of the year, on and off. An English summer is no more reliable now than it was then.

The strawberry

The history of our modern cultivated strawberry goes, like so many other good things in the kitchen garden, back to France. The wild wood strawberry (*Fragaria vesca*) was gathered where

it grew, or cultivated in both English and European gardens, since at least 1400. Around 1530 the Alpine strawberry was introduced, and this later fruiting variety prolonged the season for the gardener. The wild varieties, though good and with a long season, had small fruits. The breakthrough that was to lead to the plump, handbag-shaped monsters we admire today began in 1624 when Louis XIII's botanist Jean Robin brought the North American *Fragaria virginiana* to France. It came to England in 1727, but was unpopular – though the fruits were large, they weren't thought to be as well flavoured as the old wild berries, nor did they bear fruit for so long. The botanist Duchesne eventually clinched the breakthrough at the end of the 18th century, with a successful hybrid made by crossing the *Fragaria chiloensis* with *Fragaria virginiana* and the result was the Pine strawberry. The French Revolution disrupted its development there, but English growers took it up. Eventually in 1821, at Isleworth, Michael Keen produced his prize-winning Keen's Seedling; it was large, luscious and juicy – the modern strawberry had arrived.

Guarding the strawberries

After a delightful afternoon drinking iced claret cup and eating enormous strawberries at Clifford Priory, the Rev. Francis Kilvert and his friends had *great fun on the lawn, 6 cross games of croquet and balls flying in all directions.* More claret cup and more strawberries were followed by the *strange and solemn* sight of a total eclipse of the moon, after which everyone strolled about the terraces in different groups; *we wandered up into the twilit garden and there among the strawberries fastened to a little kennel by a collar and a light chain to keep the birds away was a most dear, delightful white pussy, very like Polar . . . he climbed my leg as if it had been a tree. Three more cats were chained to kennels near the back door.* Tuesday, July 12th, 1870.

Watering

In July the gardener is, to quote Stephen Switzer, *indeed released from all the troubles of his hot-beds; but then there are continual irrigations and waterings requisite, not only to enlarge what is now coming to perfection, but to preserve alive all those new-planted things that are design'd for the Winter.* He merely exchanges one tyranny for another. In the days before mains water came to the kitchen garden, the clatter and bustle of twelve to sixteen gardeners pushing their water carts and 'garden engines' up and down the gravel paths was enough to keep the birds and squirrels away.

It's a bad thing when the watering is insufficient. Cobbett felt strongly on this point, as on so many others. *Nothing* [is] *. . .more difficult than, behind my back, to secure an honest watering, Watering pots when full, are heavy; the distance may be* *great, and few men like to carry heavy things for any long continuation. Just turn your back, and they barely wet the ground; and if you return, you see that the strawberries have all been watered, but (and mind this) go the next day, if the weather have continued fair, and you will see then how you have been cheated.*

In Thomas Hill's *Gardener's Labyrinth* (1577) there is a fine illustration of a 'great squirt' for watering his garden. It is a kind of stirrup pump made of tin which sends water over half his garden from a portable tub. He also shows a straightforward permanently stationed pump which is positioned so that it can irrigate the whole garden by filling narrow troughs between the beds.

To keep cucumbers or melons

Cut them when they are at their best and lay them in a box made for the purpose, just to fit them. Then bury the box in dry sand, one foot deep. Don't put any moss or hay with the fruit, or it will turn yellow. (1858)

The fruit house

A well-run establishment could only be supplied with fresh fruit all the year round if there was a suitable place for storing it. The fruit house, fruit room or fruitery was used mainly for apples and pears, which by skilful management could be presented at table from July, when the first of the season's crops ripened, to May, when the last of the winter stores would be

finished. A fruit house might be no more than a bare, utilitarian shed tucked away among other outhouses, or it might be an ornamental building in the garden. Stephen Switzer's fruit room was *neither a vault, nor cellar, not yet a garret; the first will be subject to Damps, and consequently create a mustiness, and rot the Fruit, and the other will be subject to too much Air, and perhaps Sun, and that will wither it.* The ideal was a *Middle Room well ceil'd about 12 feet high with a fireplace, or some other means of heating, to fend off frost.*

In July, while the 'red fruits' were in season and when the last season's 'housed fruits' were pretty well finished, the fruit house had its annual clean-out. Shelves, drawers and walls were scrubbed, the floors swept; repairs made, cobwebs dusted away; it was aired well, then all was made ready again, with fresh linings of straw, moss or sand, for the new season's crop.

Keeping a tally of the fruit in the fruit room

By the time Loudon wrote his *Encyclopaedia* (1822), the fruit room had become quite a business-like place, not as it was formerly, *a mere loft, where fruits were kept on the floor in common with onions, with no proper means of separation, or arrangement for systematic consumption.* It was to be a long, narrow room, heated by a flue and well ventilated. He recommended solid shelves for jars and boxes of fruit, and latticed ones on which square sieve-fuls of fruit could be laid, these to range all along one side. Each jar, box and sieve was to be numbered; these numbers were also to be listed on a slate, which hung on the wall, with a space for the amounts taken to be chalked up daily. This way the house-steward could keep a check on what was available.

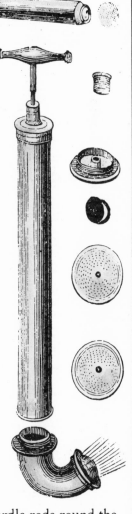

The fruit cellar

Loudon advised building this under the fruit room, with the root cellar alongside, under the office and seed shop. Both could be reached from the same staircase. If the fruit above was housed as comfortably as the master's best horses, the fruit and roots below had quarters almost good enough for his wines.

Preserving fruit on the tree

Mat up small fruits on North walls, intended to be preserved till late in the Autumn. This direction may seem strange to us, but it was the vogue in the 19th-century garden, and earlier. Cobbett directs his readers to put willow or hurdle rods round the best currants, where none of the fruit has been *fingered*, and then to lay mats over the top, or better, cover them with canvas or bunting; the crop may be preserved till October.

Loudon's calendar of fruit in season (*Encyclopaedia*, 1822) mentions that plums and morello cherries *carefully preserved on the trees* should still be available in January, as long as there were no hard frosts. He also says that gooseberries and currants will keep on the trees till Christmas, as long as they are carefully covered with mats to protect them from rain, mice, insects and

birds. The best sorts of gooseberry for this are the 'thick-skinned kind', red or yellow. Where late-fruiting currants and gooseberries are grown as espaliers on a north wall (as they often are, even today, in Northern England and Scotland) it should be quite feasible to do this – Parson Woodforde *gathered some white currants from a tree in the walled garden this day* [November 12th, 1796] *about Noon*; but perhaps modern gardeners don't have the patience to wait that long.

Cucumber glasses

Evelyn appears to be the first to mention *curcurbit glasses* by name in 1691 and at this date he calls them *new invented*. Actually he doesn't recommend using them so much for straightening cucumbers, as for holding beer mingled with honey to entice wasps and flies.

It was asserted (by male gardeners) that any woman with *the reds or her course* must not go near, or even look at a growing cucumber, or it will wither at once.

Advice to the young gardener

The young gardener should now devote a considerable portion of his time to collecting and drying specimens [of flowers] *duplicates and triplicates in order to acquire a stock to exchange with brother gardeners or naturalists; or with booksellers, apothecaries, students, schoolmasters and clergymen, for the loan of books and for aid and instruction in study.* (Loudon, 1822)

Odd jobs

Keep on destroying insects; *keep earwigs, ants, boys and idle women from fruits as cherries etc. approaching to a state of ripeness.* (Loudon, 1822)

Collect mushroom spawn. The truffle is now dug up in commons and forests. (1822)

Clear out the fruit room. If the fruit cellar still has apples and pears in it, in casks, or even some grapes still in cases, and if it gets too warm, move them to the ice house.

Have still an eye to the weeding; begin the work of Haughing as soon as ever they begin to peep; you will rid more in a few hours, than afterwards in a whole Day, whereas neglecting it till they are ready to show themselves, you do but stir and prepare for a more numerous crop of these Garden Sinns. (Evelyn, 1691)

About the middle or latter end of July . . . the greens of onions, carrots, beets, parsnips, etc. should be trod or rowl'd down with a heavy wooden or stone rowler; or else their leaves should be cut shorter, to make the roots grow bigger, by hind'ring the sap from spending itself above ground. (Switzer, 1727)

Distil and dry flowering herbs. Streighten the entrance of your Bees a little; and help them to kill their drones, if you observe too many. Give plentiful refreshment to your Mural Fruit Trees. . . feed your Vines with Blood, sweet and mingled with water . . . but as with all Summer Refreshings, is only to be done early in the Mornings, or late in the Evenings. (Evelyn, 1691)

*The Sun being now in its sou-
thern declination the Air begins to
cool, and it is become very pleasant to
walk after a thunder shower. Although the Beauties of the
Fields and Gardens begin to fade, yet the profits now flow in . . .
the Avenues and walks of your Gardens, now furnish the most
curious Palates with the most delicate Fruits, and the Kitchen
Garden the Table with variety of Tillage.* (1688)

The flower and vegetable show

*Tuesday, 30 August 1870. Hay Flower Show, the first they have
had, a very successful one. A nice large tent, the poles prettily
wreathed with hop vine, and the flowers, fruit and vegetables
prettily arranged. There was an excursion train from Builth to Hay
for the occasion. The whole country was there. A row of pretty girls,
Bevans and Thomases, were sitting on a form which broke down and
left the whole row sprawling on their backs, with their heels in the
air. Fanny Thomas was the only one who had any presence of mind
about ancles. . .* (From the Rev. Francis Kilvert's *Diary*)

This is the time for the special shows of gooseberry giants,
Yorkshire cabbages, the mammoth pot or blanched leeks and
yard-long parsnips. They form a curious sideline for the
professional gardener, who meets the amateur here on equal
terms. Somewhere out on his allotment, the amateur is digging,
slowly, sensitively, very, very carefully for his longest carrots,
feeling with his fingers in case there are any blemishes that will

make his efforts a waste of time. In the walled garden, the head gardener has a private corner for giant leeks (that will never reach his master's table), cocooned in the wife's old tights, or a piece of drain pipe.

Record gooseberry

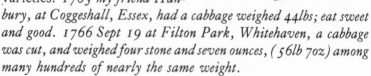

From the *Yorkshire Post* Wednesday August 12, 1978, we learn that the 178th Egton Bridge Gooseberry Show had been adversely affected by cold winds and heavy rain. However, on this occasion the champion berry weighed 21 drams 9 grains (just under 2 oz) beating a record which had stood since 1852. Prizes worth £120 included teasets, kitchen ware, linen and garden tools.

Mammoth cabbages

Peter Collinson recorded two giants in his *Memoranda* c.1766, but doesn't reveal the varieties. *1765 my friend Hanbury, at Coggeshall, Essex, had a cabbage weighed 44lbs; eat sweet and good. 1766 Sept 19 at Filton Park, Whitehaven, a cabbage was cut, and weighed four stone and seven ounces, (56lb 7oz) among many hundreds of nearly the same weight.*

Sir Francis Carew's late cherries

Beddington Park, 9 miles due south of Westminster Bridge and not far from Croydon, was not just famous for its ancient orange trees. It was also, in August 1599, the scene of a Royal visit. In the garden Elizabeth I was amazed to find a cherry tree laden with ripe fruit. The proud owner, Sir Francis Carew, then aged 69, had delayed its ripening by at least a month by covering the tree with a canvas tent. A few days before the great event he uncovered the cherries *and a few sunny days brought them to their full maturity.*

Some whoppers

The most famous seedsmen for record-beating vegetable-growers are Robinson's of Sunny Bank, Forton, near Preston. The Robinson family has raised 'Mammoth' seeds since 1860. To produce giant specimens the strain of seed has to be a kind that has the potential to produce big fruit or vegetables in the first place. *It is no good at all just buying a cheap packet of seed and hoping that it will produce a Giant.* Miss E. M. Robinson, daughter and co-director of the present head of the firm says . . . *many of the ordinary varieties that are fed and fed have poor flavour and look rather ugly, which gives Giant Veg a bad image. The good, large, prizewinner does not have to be tough or flavourless, just because it is large, the best Giants are meant to be both large and well-flavoured.*

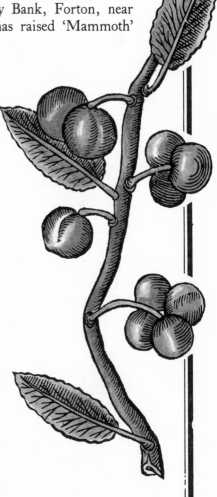

Here is a list of some of the more outstanding weights and measurements achieved by competitive vegetable growing. (Recorded in November 1981.)
Longest parsnip – 84½ inches.

Longest beetroot – 93 inches. Longest carrot – 66½ inches (all grown by a Scotsman in bottomless tubes). Heaviest marrow – 76lb 8oz. Heaviest pumpkin – 248lb (a baby compared to the world record of 493½lb, grown in Canada). Longest cucumber – 27½ inches. And so on. . .

A record length for a cucumber

Peter Collinson, in his *Memoranda* of 1766, notes *I sent seeds of a Turkey Cucumber to Mr Custis in Virginia, in the year 1737. It produced a fruit three feet long and fourteen inches round; grew in one night three inches in length, and people came twenty miles round to visit it. Such are the effects of so fine a climate on so rich a soil.*

The 1981 *Garden News* record for the longest British cucumber was 27½ inches, and the heaviest was 11lb 2oz.

Pears in a bottle

William pears are still grown in bottles in kitchen gardens in Northern France. When they are ripe, the pears and bottles are detached from the trees where they have hung since the fruit was embryonic and the bottles are filled with the delicious liqueur 'Poire William'. This is the secret of how a fully grown pear (like a fully rigged ship) gets into a narrow-necked bottle.

The naming of a nectarine

Captain Leonard Gurle (c. 1621-85) was a famous nurseryman in Hoxton, (then known as Hogsden). His nursery covered about 12 acres of what is now part of Whitechapel, one of the grittiest areas in the East End of London. It takes quite an effort as you walk down Brick Lane Market to envisage green and peaceful acres of seedlings there, circa 1660. It was here that the famous Elrouge nectarine was raised; a hardy variety which still appears in some nurserymen's lists. At first Gurle called it the Elrug, which is his own name spelt backwards, but this was later softened to Elrouge, and Gurle also began to spell his own name as 'Gourle'.

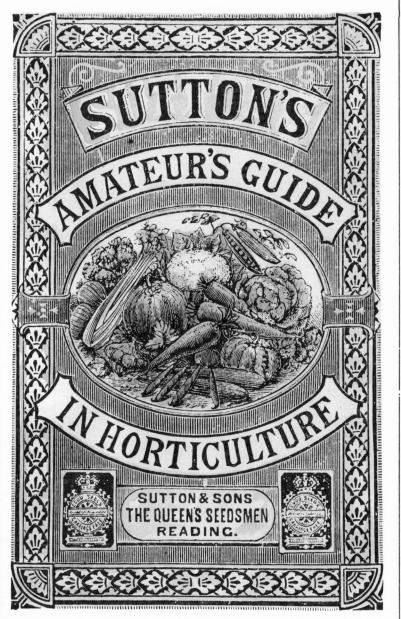

SUTTON'S

AMATEUR'S GUIDE

IN HORTICULTURE

SUTTON & SONS
THE QUEEN'S SEEDSMEN
READING.

Onion mammoths

Mammoth exhibition onions have been a mania with competitive gardeners for at least 50 years. Instructions for their cultivation can now be heard on a tape made and sold by the Robinsons. The family firm was founded in 1860, and their seed onions have been grown on the same bed since 1890, which must be a record in itself, for an onion bed.

Like most records of a competitive kind, the record size for onions increases every year. In 1920 a 2lb onion was thought a marvel; in the thirties a 4 pounder would inspire awe; today's national champions are approaching 7½lbs. (At the time of writing, the national record of 7lbs 6oz., won by a Galashiels man in 1981, is still unbroken) while 5lb prize winners, with 22-inch girths are quite usual at any humble village flower and vegetable show. Red or white, they are said to be just as good to eat as any normal, everyday onion. The problem of how to eat 7lbs of onion at one go need not arise if you take Mr Robinson's daughter's advice. These onions keep very well once peeled; the cook should therefore peel the whole thing and use it by instalments, detaching the required amount layer by layer, until it's all been eaten.

'A strange use for a cowcumber'

Hugh Plat published this notion in *Delightes for Ladies*, 1602; he says it is an *Italian conceipt . . . to catch the flyes that would otherwise deface the pictures*. It looks very comical but, when I tried it, it attracted no flies. *Pricke a cowcumber full of barley cornes with the small spiring ends outward. Make little holes in the cowcumber first, with a wooden or bone bodkin, and after put in the graine. These being thick placed will in time cover all the cowcumber, so as no man can discerne what strange plant the same should bee. Such cowcumbers are to be hung up in the middest of summer roomes to draw all flies unto them, which otherwise would flie upon pictures or hangings.*

Advice to the young gardener

Insects, especially the winged tribes, now abound; and the young gardener should be assiduous in collecting them for the same object as

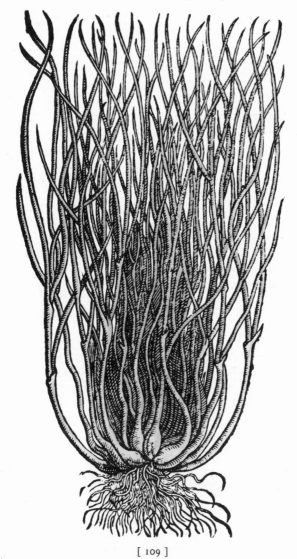

he collects specimen plants. By carrying a small box in his pocket, he may pick them up while at work. (Loudon, 1822)

Odd jobs

Little is now to be done in a Garden, besides gathering in the Fruits of former Labours. (1688)

Make your Summer Perry and Cider; pull up ripe onions and garlick, etc. Clip Herbs within one handful of the ground; Innoculate buds, if you have not begun already. Vindemiate, and take your Bees towards the expiration of this Month. (1691)

Gather lettuce seed and keep each sort separate, also seeds of Chiboul [spring onion]*, Onion, Beet. Leave it in its cod till you want to sow it, then rub it out. You can beat it with Pestle and Mortar without hurting it. Roll onions, to stop them growing. Pull leaves off wall-Fruit for the sun to reach in, to ripen Peaches and Pears. Gather all pease designed for Winter store. Dig borders, clean alleys.* (1706)

Weed the fruit borders very well, as it looks not only very neat, but also reflects more heat on to the fruit on the walls, from the bare earth. Net trees, hang vials in trees to catch wasps. (1779)

Search for mushroom spawn in horse and cow pastures. (1822)

The moderate temperature of the air . . . invites the inhabitants

of cities and confin'd places to sally out and breath the free air of the country; and tho' there are a great many curiosities of the garden past and gone, yet there remains some pease and beans, an abundance of artichokes, some collyflowers and fruits are yet in plenty; so that in fine, such is the coolness, serenity and silence of these two months (especially October) that I can't think it excelled by any one of the twelve. (Switzer, *Practical Kitchen Gardener*, 1727)

This season is the most pleasant of all the year for Air, it being generally of an even temperature, by Night as well as by Day . . . the sweetest time of all the Year for travelling, walking and such like Champaign Exercises. (J. W., 1688)

Almost all is in the state of decline and in activity here, as regards the forcing ground, but: in the greenhouse *Ha! we smell winter here.* (Cobbett, 1833)

A kitchen garden in Ireland

He pushed open the door, then followed her into the garden which, deep in its walls, seemed impossibly large, for one could not see to the end of it: it was crossed by espaliers and crowded with apple-trees. Down the borders, the September yellow and scarlets were metallic in unsunny light. Dahlias, orange and wine-coloured blazed and gloomed. He turned down one path, she kept to the other; they silently parted. Here she had come with Marda . . . they had sat on

[113]

the green seat, pressed blisters out of the paint and spat out their plum-stones into the box border opposite. (The Last September by Elizabeth Bowen, 1929)

The cardoon

This plant looks very like a globe artichoke, but it is not grown for its heads which are small, tough and tasteless. It is grown for its leaf stems, which grow 4 to 6 feet high and when blanched make a most delicious, tender, delicate and tasty vegetable, not unlike celery or Swiss chard stems. Yet the cardoon appears to be just as unknown now in this country as it was in 1629, when Parkinson wrote: *John Tradescante assured me, hee saw three*

Acres of land about Brussels planted with this kinde of artichoke, which the owner whited like Endive, and then sold them in the Winter; Wee cannot yet finde the true manner of dressing them, that our country may delight therein.

A curious feature of the cardoon flowerhead is that the soft 'choke', when dry, can be infused in water then used as a sort of rennet to make milk curdle for cheese or junket. The French and the Spaniards are said to use it in this way. I tried to do it, but failed, possibly because my milk was pasteurised. The cook is warned in some gardening books not to touch milk directly after handling artichokes or it will curdle, but I have never heard of this actually happening.

The tomato or love apple

The tomato had been cultivated here since the late 16th century as an ornamental plant; no-one ate the fruit very much till late in the 18th century. This seems odd, as travellers to Italy, France, Spain and Portugal could hardly avoid noticing the preponderance of the tomato there, in salads, soups, sauces and 'ragoos'. Eating the tomato raw, even on the Continent, came later still.

On December 27th, 1884, *The Gardener's Chronicle* reports: *It is often said that people may get used to anything, in the matter of what they eat included, and there is no denying the fact that an acquired taste is necessary to make some things at all palatable – Tomatoes to wit. The flavour of this vegetable is so different to that of everything else, and until recent times it was comparatively so little known, that there was little demand for them, yet the way people take to eating the juicy red fruit, raw or cooked, after a few trials of it, is surprising . . .*

To remove the stains of mulberries

The juice of the fruit when ripe, that is – when the berry is black, will stain the hands, but that of the unripe fruit, which is white, will remove the marks. Pliny, Book XV chapter 27. This is perfectly true. I tried it out on the fruit of an ancient mulberry at Albury Park and the gardener there told me it was similar to a trick that also worked with tomatoes. After picking a large quantity your hands become stained dark green, almost black. If you rub them with an unripe tomato, cut in half, before washing, they become quite clean. Hugh Plat recommends the juice of sorrel as an all-purpose stain remover, 1602.

The scarlet runner bean

Like tomatoes, runner beans were not originally grown for their fruits, or pods, but for ornament. It was their climbing habit (unchecked they will grow as high as hops) and bright red flowers that made them desirable. They were thought a touch too vulgar for great parterres or flower gardens, but were welcomed in *little courts* where they formed shady arbours, or tunnelled alleys, or were *made to cover any defects in our walls.* They were originally introduced (from Mexico) by Henry Compton (1632-1713) the Bishop of London, who had a famous garden at Fulham Palace, in the mid-17th century. In 1677 they appear in a seedsman's catalogue among flowers, between *lupines* and *everlasting pease.* It was not until 1731 that any gardening writer mentioned boiling the *cods.*

Vegetable marrows

Large vegetable marrows make me sad. Firstly, they mean autumn has come; secondly, they are inedible. Most gardening books agree that they were very little grown here before 1816, when the first seeds of the *Cucurbita succada* or Cicader were brought by ships from the East Indies. Yet, even as late as 1850, J. C. Loudon's *Encyclopaedia*, usually an unfailing fountain of knowledge, gives no instruction for their cultivation. It appears not to have been described in detail till 1865 when William Rhind, in his *History of the Vegetable Kingdom* writes: *the vegetable marrow or Cucurbita succada is but lately introduced in this country, it is straw coloured, of an oval or elongated shape, and when fully grown attains the length of about nine inches.* Gilbert White first grew them in 1760, in the same bed as his melons. They proved to be *very fleshy and high-flavoured* and they fruited continuously from June to October.

The mushroom stone

In 185 BC Nicander refers to *rarified muds from the core of the earth* which can generate mushrooms. Almost 1,000 years later they crop up again, this time in the form of *a Stone in the*

possession of the Right Honourable the Earl of Stafford, which on being WATERED produces excellent mushrooms. It came either from Piedmont, Naples or Sicily and is described in detail by Dr John Hill, in 1758, in a tract on the *lapis fungifer,* or mushroom stone. In reality it appears to have been no more than an extremely hard, almost ossified piece of mushroom spawn, looking rather like a piece of volcanic rock.

Picking fruit

Peaches, apricots, nectarines and plums should be picked with a peach gatherer, which is a tin funnel lined with velvet. This gadget is recommended by Loudon in 1830. Failing that, the gardener should wear soft cotton gloves when picking fruit with a bloom on it. *Peaches* and *nectarines* could be left a fortnight on the tree after ripening, as long as they were covered up.

Figs are ready to be gathered *when you observe a tear, as it were of Syrop standing in the Eye. When they are gather'd, which must not be in the Heat of the Sun, you must lay 'em sideways in a Basket with leaves. You must let 'em lye one night in the Fruitery, and the next Day they will eat fresh . . . When they are served in at table they must lye in the same manner as in the Fruitery.* (London and Wise, 1706)

If you would preserve your Plums with the Blue upon 'em, you must lay 'em when gather'd in a basket among the leaves of Nettles;

you must never take them out for fear of rubbing off the Blue . . .
(London and Wise, 1706)

Gather apples and pears when full ripe, especially those for keeping, or for cyder, in a dry day, clear, but not frostie, in large baskets, lin'd with straw-mats, upon three footed or standing ladders; at least lay straw under, if you shake them, and suffer not too many at once therein. (John Reid. *The Scots Gard'ner*, 1683)

Gather not your pippins till the full Moon after Michelmas (September 29th); so you may keep them a whole yeare without shrinking; and so of the grapes, and all other fruits; so of onion seeds, annis seeds, and other seed, which you would keep full and plump. (Hugh Plat, *Garden of Eden*, 1653, 4th edition)

Gather apples after the autumnal equinox [21 Sept] *but never begin before the sixteenth day of the moon.* (Pliny)

The ripening of *melons* is so critical that the gardener should *not fail to visit the melonry at least three times a day, morning, noon and evening.* Having cut one, it should not be eaten immediately, but kept for twenty-four hours *in some sweet, dry, place.*

Beating the wasps

By now wasps and gardeners are at the peak of their battle against one another. All the fruit house ventilators are open, but protected by gauze. On the fruit walls and in the orchard every prize fruit about to ripen is clothed in a little muslin or paper bag. In Switzer's time there were *little square glasses made about London, about as big as a large bunch* [of grapes] *but these in windy weather are apt to break; the cheapest method is the dipping of whited-brown paper bags in Sweet Oil, and putting the bunches when dry therein, and this will preserve them a great while, even till Christmas in a mild time, and will keep the wet from them a great while.* (1752)

Gilbert White had a bad time with wasps ten years later, *Sept. 8. 1762. The wasps (which are without number this dry, hot summer) attack the grapes in a grievous manner. Hung up 16 bottles*

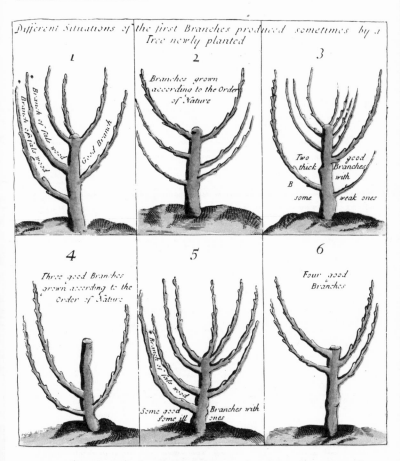

Different Situations of the first Branches produced sometimes by a Tree newly planted

1

Branch of false wood
Branch of false wood
Good Branch

2

Branches grown according to the Order of Nature

3

Two thick
B
some
good Branches with
weak ones

4

Three good Branches grown according to the Order of Nature

5

Branch of false wood
Some good
Branches with some ill ones

6

Four good Branches

with treacle and beer which make a great havock among them. Bagged about fifty of the best bunches in Grape-Bags. Some of the forward bunches are very eatable tho' not curiously ripe. Mr Snooke's grapes were eat naked to the stones a fortnight ago, when they were quite green.

Advice to the young gardener

The young gardener should make drawings of apples and pears in a notebook, when he can afford time from other studies.

Odd jobs

Gather now (if ripe) your winter fruits, as Apples, Pears, Plums, etc. to prevent their falling by the great Winds: also gather your Wind-falls from day to day: do this work in dry weather. Prepare compost. No longer defer the taking of your Bees, strengthening the entrances of such Hives as you leave to a small passage, and continue still your hostility against Wasps, and other robbing insects. About Michaelmas retire your choice greens and rarest Plants into your Conservatory. (1691) Take all the wet days and convenient opportunities . . . for roping onions and tying garlick, shallots and rocambole up in bunches, to hang in the chimney during winter, in as much as that will preserve them better than lying on a floor. (1727)

Gather almond, peach and plum stones . . . towards the end gather saffron. (1683)

Stick, stop, support, cut down, blanch, and thin where you see it necessary; no time is to be lost at this season. Take up potatoes, gather nasturtium seeds for pickling. With the forcing house and greenhouse at rest, it is time to repair, reglaze, paint; clean the flues. (1830)

It can *often be very favour-able, which gives a great opportunity to the gardener for planting of trees . . . but sometimes it happens that the Frost sets in early in this month, which occasions a great deal of trouble to get his plants shelter'd and his winter Fruits gather'd . . . be directed by the difference of the seasons.* (1731)

The tortoise now begins to bury himself in the ground. (1830)

October 18, 1759. The mornings begin to be frosty, yet ye grapes continue in high perfection. October 12, 1765. Snakes are still abroad and wood ants are creeping about. A great rain again last night. October 26, 1765. A very white frost this morning. I have seen no swallows since the 15th. (Gilbert White, *Garden Kalendar*)

How fruit was stored

Lay them in drye places, in drye strawe or hey . . . or in a barley mowe not touching the other, or in chaffe, and in vessels of Juniper or Sypers [cypress] *wood, ye may keep them well in dry salt or hony, and upon bordes where a fyre is nighe all the wynter, also hanging nie fyre in the wynter, in nettes of yarne.* (Leonard Mascall, 1572)

Fruit that would not keep well, such as cherries or plums, was preserved in wine, cider, honey or sugar, or dried in the oven.

To keepe Peares a year . . . put them in a barrell with fine salt

*very dry . . . in such sort that one Peare doe not touch another, to
fill the barrell . . . stoppe it and let it be set in some dry place, that
the salt do not waxe moist . . .* (1572)

To keep nuts

There are several ways – all of these were suggested by Leonard
Mascall, in 1572: *in dry sande in a dry bladder, or in a fatte* [vat]
*made of Walnut tree, and put of dry Ivie berries therein, and they
shall be much sweeter. To keep Nuttes green a yeare and also freshe
. . . put them in a pot with hony . . . and the sayde hony will be
gentle and good for many medecines . . . Keep walnuts fresh and
greene in the time of strayning of verjuice* [the juice of unripe

grapes], *ye shall take that pommis and put therof in the bottome of a
barrell, in layers until the barrell is full, then stop him close and put
him in a sellar . . . Some fill an earthen pot with small nuttes, then
put in dry sand, make a lid of earth or stone, then clay it and put it
upside down, two feete within the Earthe . . .*

To keep potatoes

Cobbett hated the potato for political as well as culinary reasons. *To raise potatoes for the purpose of being used instead of bread, is a thing mischievious to the nation.* He declared it to be inferior food for cattle or pigs as well; both animals fare much better on cabbages, swedes or mangel-wurzels. As for eating the potato; *it does very well to qualify the effects of fat meat, or to assist in the swallowing of quantities of butter* . . . but he says he never ate it himself, finding *other things far preferable.* However, he gives instructions for growing and keeping them; they should be

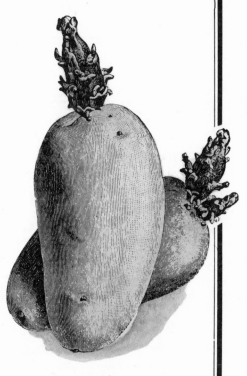

lifted in late October and when dry and clean, stored in a cellar or barn or otherwise frost-free place. *If you can ascertain the degree of warmth just necessary to keep a baby from perishing from cold, you know precisely the precautions required to preserve a potato above-ground.* From this he appears to dislike babies almost as much as potatoes.

A record crop of potatoes

In October, 1746 Peter Collinson dug up one potato root which he had planted *in rich soil in Spring.* It had 101 potatoes on it, small and great. In October 1766 a gardener at Ely had from one root, 19 score (380) of potatoes, the size of cricket balls, and many more the size of marbles.

The orangery, 1703

About the middle of October it is time to bring your oranges back into their conservatory, greenhouse or orangery. *Choose a clear dry day, that their leaves may be thoroughly dry, yet so that a gentle Rain may have washed all the Dust from the leaves.* If the cases holding the plants were not too heavy, they were lifted by poles slung under hooks on the boxes. Heavy boxes were moved *with a long rowling Engine drawn by horses.* They were spaced out to leave enough room for watering, and the prospect was rendered more agreeable by placing in the middle, and upon the sides of walls and on pedestals some *by-plants* such as *Jesmins, Myrtles, Laurels, etc.* Pots of water were put about, so that rats and mice *will quell their thirst and so be kept from the Trees, which they would otherwise injure, by sucking their moisture.* These water pots also acted as indicators for the temperature. If it was too cold the trees were warmed with burning lamps, *but not so close as to burn the leaves.*

The ideal orangery should answer on five points: 1) It must be sunny; 2) It should have plenty of windows that close well; 3) It should have thick, firm walls; 4) It should have a good ceiling; 5) It must not be hollow under the floor. Also: the doors must be wide enough to carry trees in and out. The windows, running from a 3 foot high *breastwork* to the ceiling, must be 5-6 feet wide, so that plenty of warmth and light reaches the trees in Winter. They should be double sealed with oiled paper inside, and glazed outside. Wooden shutters are not good, as they *cheat many lovers of flowers.* The walls must be at least 2½ feet thick, and can be of loam mixed with reeds, or double-deal filled with earth and sand, if bricks are dear. The north side should have other buildings, a dry hill, or a wood and tall trees, behind it. The roof, which will have an attic in it, must be insulated with hay or straw if it is not lived in. The floor *can never be too dry.* It should be of hard earth, plaster or boards, with no cellars or vaults below as they harbour damp. The

dimensions of this ideal orangery are 24 x 36 feet. One of the oldest orangeries in the country is still to be seen, at Chatsworth. It was built in 1697-8 by the first Duke of Devonshire. The orangery at Kensington Palace was built in 1705.

Cucumber seed

If cucumber seed be steeped all night in water, mixed with cow-dung, and sown in a hot-bed, even in October, it will come up the third day; if in the Spring, earlier. (1795)

Advice to the young gardener

A few specimens of plants may still be collected, and many species from the animal kingdom. Not one animated being should be neglected from the worm upwards. Collections of spiders are best made this month, and the young gardener may continue to dissect and study the pulpy fruits. (1822)

Odd jobs

All but the latest fruit is picked and stored away; the apple house and root cellar are full; the ground is clear or only sparsely tenanted. Rhubarb, asparagus and seakale leaves are becoming brittle; the palisades of runner beans begin to show bare poles.